The Transformation of Consciousness in Myth

The Reshaping of Psychoanalysis
From Sigmund Freud to Ernest Becker

Barry R. Arnold
General Editor

Vol. 4

PETER LANG
New York • San Francisco • Bern • Baltimore
Frankfurt am Main • Berlin • Wien • Paris

John W. Tigue

The Transformation of Consciousness in Myth

Integrating the Thought of Jung and Campbell

PETER LANG
New York • San Francisco • Bern • Baltimore
Frankfurt am Main • Berlin • Wien • Paris

BF
175.5
.M95
T54
1993

Library of Congress Cataloging-in-Publication Data

Tigue, John W.
    The transformation of consciousness in myth: integrating the thought of Jung and Campbell/ John W. Tigue.
       p.   cm. — (The reshaping of psychoanalysis; vol.4)
       1. Myth—Psychological aspects. 2. Archetype (Psychology). 3. Jung, C. G. (Carl Gustav), 1875–1961. 4. Campbell, Joseph, 1904–
I. Title. II. Series.
BF175.5.M95T54   1994   291.1'3'019—dc20   93-12339
ISBN 0-8204-2130-8   CIP
ISSN 1059-3551

Die Deutsche Bibliothek-CIP-Einheitsaufnahme

Tigue, John W.:
The transformation of consciousness in myth: integrating the thought of Jung and Campbell / John W. Tigue. - New York; Berlin; Bern; Frankfurt/M.; Paris; Wien: Lang, 1994
  (The reshaping of psychoanalysis; Vol. 4)
  ISBN 0-8204-2130-8
NE: GT

Cover design by James F. Brisson.

The paper in this book meets the guidelines for permanence and durability of the Committee on Production Guidelines for Book Longevity of the Council on Library Resources.

© Peter Lang Publishing, Inc., New York 1994

All rights reserved.
Reprint or reproduction, even partially, in all forms such as microfilm, xerography, microfiche, microcard, offset strictly prohibited.

Printed in the United States of America.

Table of Contents

Acknowledgements vii

Introduction 1

Chapter One
The Symbol's Journey:
Archetypal Expression 19

Chapter Two
The Symbol's Appearance:
Mythography 33

Chapter Three
The Symbol's Personhood:
Heroes 47

Chapter Four
The Epic of Gilgamesh 55

Chapter Five
Bhagavad Gita 73

Chapter Six
Owein 91

Chapter Seven
Star Wars 105

Chapter Eight
The Feminine Presence in Myths:
An Ethical Imperative 121

Conclusion 135

Bibliography 145

Acknowledgements

I am most appreciative to Dr. David Darst, Dr. Justin Glenn, Dr. Leon Golden, and Dr. Charles Muenchow for their suggestions and comments which brought about a greater clarification of my ideas. Additionally, I wish to recognize Dr. Charles R. Warth for his gifted insights into the human psyche. John Tigue has published portions of this manuscript, in part, in the following journals:

"El Miedo de la Feminidad Como un Resulto de la Evolución del Consciente. *Síntoma*, 2 (March 1993).

"Teaching Mythology as a Subtext of the Humanities." *J. of General Education*, 41 (Spring 1993).

"Star Wars, Archetypes, and the Mythic Quest." *The Quest*, 5.1 (Spring 1992).

I should like to dedicate this book to my parents, John and Kim Tigue, for their love, encouragement, and support throughout my life.

Introduction

My study will focus primarily on the elementary ideas or archetypes as expressed in myths. This will involve a detailed discussion of the nature of archetypes, their relationship with the unconscious, their transformation in the human psyche, and their relationship with the human organism. According to Carl Jung, archetypes are the mental images of the human body, the pictures which seek to bring order to its biochemical systems. They are the motive forces in people's lives guiding them toward their destinies. Myths provide a medium for objectifying these mental images and, therefore, are a good source of archetypal images. Myths are a narrative objectification of unconscious processes and their attempt at finding expression in consciousness. I shall thus be examining how archetypes function as pathways to the unconscious and how myths permit the requisite insight into their relevancy. This insight should ostensibly be applied to people's everyday experiences and lived out in their lives. When the latent content of archetypes in myths becomes a manifestation of people's conscious stream of activities, it brings about a transformation of consciousness. That is, the formless archetypes seek to bond with consciousness, thus becoming embodied. At this point, people now have the opportunity to make contact with the archetypes and work cooperatively with them, thus fostering psychic integration.

Specifically, then, I shall examine the concept of archetypes, explain the power of the symbols and the metaphors which are the voices of the archetypes and form the content of myths, to justify the effective role myths play as a teaching mechanism, as well as providing a way for a deeper understanding of human beings and their development.

Prior to summarizing the content of each chapter, I should like to discuss my reasoning on why I have chosen to integrate the conceptual theories of Carl Jung and Joseph Campbell. The series' title in which this book is included is *Reshaping of Psychoanalysis: From Freud to Becker*. I feel privileged to have been able to add to this reshaping. My initial influence in exploring the human psyche was through the writings of Sigmund Freud. His theories were useful in providing me with tools to reflect on how my inner world was interacting with my outer world. Freudian psychology allowed me to tune in to my own psychic energies and gain greater control over my emotions. Analyzing myself allowed me greater freedom and flexibility to develop my potentials. I was less hindered by emotional annoyances and, thus, used the greater clarity of my perception to accomplish the task at hand.

My purpose in writing about the Freud-Jung connection is to elucidate upon how Jungian thought extends and reshapes Freudian thought. The examples that I am giving are already well researched, and regarded by many post-Freudians, particularly those who cater to Jungian thought, as standing on firm ground.

I early on appreciated Jung for the positive and life-affirming comments he made about human beings. I am a strong believer in positive thinking and the productivity of working with visual imagery. Jungian psychology seemed to support my own experiences with these practices better than that of Freudian psychology. Thus, I began to move more into theories about universal wholeness, interdependence, and connectivity. Freud dealt with people as biological beings, who were conditioned by their instinctive impulses and environment. Certainly, this is an aspect of what it is to be human, but Freud failed to account for the transcendental and spiritual ambiences.

Freud's views on human nature are strongly mechanistic and empirical. Mullahy points out, if human beings are to be explained according to classical mechanics, then how can "purpose, consciousness, and the unconscious, which are qualities and modes of experience and behavior, not physical entities," (320) be accounted for?

It is obvious from reading *The Future of an Illusion* that Freud did not believe in a God, and thought that such icons acted as crutches for the weak-minded. God became simply a reflection of the conflicts between the id, ego, and superego. Freud thought religion acted as a substitute for a return to a childlike dependence on a father-ideal. In the religious circle this father ideal became god. The child or the adult invented such a father-image to make life more liveable (Frey-Rohn 53). Freud connected religion to a mass repression. Jung, on the other hand, viewed repression not as the result of the tension between drives, but as a stepping stone to developing consciousness (*Ibid* 57-58).

It is Jung who recognized the God-image as resulting from intrapsychic exchanges of cosmic energies within individuals. Freud further stated that God-images are mental constructs resulting from the resynthesis of children's ideas of their parents (Rizzuto 14-15). Freud wrote that "psychoanalysis has made people familiar with the intimate connexion between the father-complex and belief in God; it has shown them that a personal God is, psychologically, nothing other than an exalted father" (*SE* 11: 123). A particular failure of this idea is that Freud did not mention how this father-image influences young girls' conceptions (Rizzuto 15). Jung, on the other hand, wrote elaborately on the anima, Mother Goddess, and other female archetypal images, and their place and function in the human psyche. Freud was also limited in his exploration of cultural differences. He did not explain why some believe in a God while others do not. Nor for instance why the basic tenets of Buddhism and Taoism have no God-image. If God images are supposed to come from identifying with the father, then how is it that many have no image of God, and for others that image is stronger as a female presence! Societies were not always patrilineal. In fact, according to Knaster's understanding of Gimbutas, most archeological evidence seems to suggest the contrary, that matrilineal societies were dominant for quite a time (38). Freud's ideas clearly fail to consider and integrate a feminine principle. Jung clearly remedies this oversight.

Because Freud believed that God and the Devil were created from a paternal-image that split, his emphasis is on some Being imaged external to persons. Jung took these images and placed them inside the psyche as archetypal energies to be recognized, reconciled, and integrated. Freud implied that people inherit the sins of their forefathers and that they suffer an "eternal return" to the mind of primitive man. He did not supply a theory as to how to break this cycle, whereas Jung did through individuation. Besides, there is no explanation provided as to why females should inherit the patriarchal God-image when males did the crime.

Freud wrote about emotional dispositions being established early in children's lives. Jung extended this idea back further, connecting it with the archetypal powers of the collective unconscious. It is interesting that both Freud and Jung changed their ideas regarding the unconscious over the years. Freud, at first, viewed it as being analogous to that which is repressed. Later, he realized that what is repressed is indeed unconscious, but everything that is unconscious is not necessarily repressed (*SE* 19: 18). He also connected the unconscious with the id, that which is most instinctual and archaic. Developing from the id comes the ego and from it the superego. The ego has to regulate and maintain a balance between the instinctual demands of the id, the moral censoring of the superego, and the environment. For Freud the ego was the seat of anxiety, and no wonder with all that it has to do to keep all in balance. Jung, likewise, saw the ego as that which kept people safe from unpredictable unconscious energies, but not as the seat of anxiety (Frey-Rohn 112-113). Furthermore, Jung thought that the ego serviced the integrating of the unconscious, with consciousness furthering individuation.

Furthering Jung's journey into the unconscious was Campbell. He applied Jung's theories of the archetypes and collective unconscious to charting the territory of myths. So doing, he provided ample support for Jung giving credence to his theories. As Campbell strongly advocated Jung, integrating their thought was a logical connection. Freud regarded culture as negative, suppressing and inhibiting the contact people have with their environment (Mullahy 321-322). Whereas Campbell regarded the mesocosm as integral to human well-being and psychological fulfillment. There is a creative exchange of energies between individuals and their external havens. Thus Campbell is supportive of cultivating a relationship with nature, not suppressing, conquering, nor subduing it. I believe Campbell's perspective is gentler, and makes more sense, as it promotes growth and stability, not decay and chaos. Alfred Adler was at times another somewhat pessimistic theorist with his stress on the "will to power urge." He failed to realize that some persons are happy and healthy because of the nurturing environments in which they were raised. As Mullahy states, not all children grow up with inferiority complexes (324). Jung stressed healthy emotional interacting between family members, not sexual sublimation as being the root of psychological development. According to Mullahy, Karen Horney reinforces Jung and Campbell's views that culture is fundamental to activating human creative potentials (328-329). The environment is able to provide the necessary ingredients for unleashing the power within. People need to realize that the outer world is a part of themselves as much as they are a part of it. They can be mutually supportive.

What Freud did was to awaken people to a different reality. A world of motive forces, drives, desires, and wishes. Mental illness was no longer regarded as demon possession or the turning into a witch. It was recognized as an imbalance of psychic energies and misdirected libidinal urges. These were potentially within the control of the clients, and not something to which they had to remain blind. Psychoanalysis was Freud's method by which individuals could reach down into their inner chambers shining the light of reason on these mysterious forces. Thus, the hands that rocked the cradle could at last be held. Jung developed this process further when he recognized that the inner world was not always a place of contending but complimentary forces. The libido was more than a sexual impulse, it was forward moving, guiding people to a possible transcendental encounter. It was a biological urge with spiritual possibilities. And thus, the reductionistic tendency of Freud was replaced by something always in flux, changing, and progressing.

Beatrice Hinkle summarized this view on Jung's Analytical psychology, having wrote that it seeks to unify and appreciate the many aspects of human life. It places people in relationship with all organisms and the world, of which the harmonious encountering leads to greater healthy-mindedness and peace (254).

Finally, if Campbell is to be pursued with serious scholarly interest, it is necessary to scrutinize his conceptual systems is mainstream academia. His popular appeal is not a negation of his ideas, but a revelation of the hunger by the masses to be nourished psychologically. Pop psychology and New Age trends often explore regions those in academia view with suspicion and trepidation. Thus, works of genius sometimes go unnoticed because they fail to fall into normative categories. And people like Campbell, though traditional himself, are occasionally placed in this category and looked at askance, primarily because they are popular. I am in hopes that my approach of placing Campbell with the psychoanalytic tradition, as an extension of it, teamed up with Jung, will be a bridge between his popularism and traditionalism. It is a mistake to dismiss Campbell primarily on the basis of his popular appeal, as his ideas make the imagination soar, freeing it to contact places which simultaneously revitalize and unite the psyche's energies. He, like Jung, touch the feelings in people in ways that pure intellectualism is incapable of doing.

Now, I should like to begin a synopsis of each chapter. The first chapter is entitled "The Symbol's Journey: Archetypal Expression." It begins with an explanation of Carl Jung's concept of the psyche, which "has a structurally determined capacity for translating physical processes into archetypal forms" (Jacobi 47). Jung divides the psyche into the unconscious and consciousness. My focus concerns itself with a subdivision of the unconscious referred to as the "collective unconscious" and its relationship with consciousness. The idea is that the archetypes of the collective unconscious must find expression in consciousness, thus enabling human beings to integrate better the opposing tendencies of the psyche. The collective unconscious is the storage house, the great universal library of all the experiences of the human race, and I believe of all manifestations of creation. The collective unconscious uses archetypes to direct the cousin of matter, energy. Matter which becomes self-conscious learns that it is this primordial and universal energy. As the personal and collective experiences of human beings change over time, so too, is matter transformed. Hence, human beings are quite unlikely the end of cosmic evolution (Harding *I & Not-I* 204).

The experiences of human beings, as well as their ancestors, reflect the transformation of consciousness. The actions of those who walked before present day humans make their journeys easier in the same way that once one person broke the four minute mile, others readily followed. Ken Keyes wrote that when a critical number of individuals gain a specific degree of awareness, "this new awareness may be communicated from mind to mind" (17). It is in this way that human ancestors have been helping people: they taught consciousness a better way to work with matter. Put another way, the unconscious has learned the best combinations to which matter responds to integrate the archetypes. Likewise, consciousness is learning to assimilate the archetypes with greater clarity and precision. Furthermore, spirit is busy working with matter, and transforming it, to create a more complete vehicle to express through.

As a pebble (intention) breaks the surface of the water, it produces a disturbance on the surface (consciousness) which expands in ever increasing circles, like the concentric rings of an onion. This is the increase of awareness. As the pebble sinks deeper into the water, (unconscious) the awareness expands. Unfortunately, for many people, the pebble hits a stump (close-mindedness) as it begins penetration of the water's surface, or is swallowed by a fish (greed), or the storm (material distractions) on the surface interferes with the concentric waves and throws them into disarray. The solution to transforming consciousness is to confront reality by learning to recognize the projections of the unconscious and to complete the inner journey which is participated in outwardly. This recognition and participation takes place through clarification of emotional experiences, and the situations in which they occur. Recognition tends to occur by meditating on the feeling-tone of these experiences. Participation occurs through changing the behavior patterns. By patterns, I mean the repetitive emotional responses to people, places, things, and ideas. The changing of destructive patterns allows for new archetypal images to reveal themselves, and thus furthers the individuating of the psyche.

Next, I shall trace the historical development of the archetypes, and further, describe what they are, how they function, and their purposefulness. Following this, I shall look at the role of symbols and metaphors as being the language of archetypes. They provide the corporeal existence for the archetypal processes. The energy behind the archetypes affects people's lives all the time. Without symbols, people would be unable to recognize the particular processes occurring within their psyches, and thus be the unsuspecting pawns of the psyche's drama. Recognizing archetypes, through the process of translating symbols, is the doorway to the unconscious.

Chapter Two is called "The Symbol's Appearance: Mythography." I explore what myths are through various categories of interpretation proposed by, at present, some of the prominent theorists, and then examine how they function. Basically, I present the major theories on myths to expose the readers to numerous options. I am not exhaustive in my presentation and wish only to classify the most frequently used methodologies. For a more complete survey of mythic methodologies, I should suggest reading *Mythography: The Study of Myths and Rituals* by W. G. Doty and *Approaches to Greek Myth* edited by Lowell Edmunds. The psychological theories of myths, in particular those of Joseph Campbell, will serve as my methodology for discussing the function of myths. The psychological function of myths provides a pragmatic answer to many people's psychological and emotional dilemmas. Other interpretations of mythic function, though useful in their own context, do not serve to promote the Jungian notion of psychic completeness.

Chapter Three is "The Symbol's Personhood: Heroes." Here, I deal with the idea that there are certain patterns within human beings that are the same all over the world and throughout all epochs. These patterns follow certain predetermined stages regarding the development of heroic types. According to Campbell, these stages are departure, initiation, and return. Departure is where the would-be heroes or heroines, being dissatisfied with the state of things, decide to set out into personally unknown territory. This requires a great deal of courage and spirit of adventure, as this decision means breaking with cultural and social norms. Initiation is the encounters they have with ominous forces, tests, and trials of all magnitudes. This is the forest journey, the encounter with all that is dark and frightening in the world, when in reality the darkness are the souls of these journeyers, which must be turned to the light. By "soul," I am referring to the life-affirming principle that inspires sentient beings to fulfill their potentials and complete their journeys. Return is where the heroic participants come back into the old world with a new world view, a gift of sorts. The gift may be a thing, a message of a new teaching or the giving to the world of themselves as newly awakened human beings. Additionally, these stages of the heroic journey repeat the pattern on a spiritual level of higher value. The first round of adventures precede on the physical plane of life. The second round is usually of an emotional and intellectual encounter with the world. The third round continues to include the previous rounds as well as being a journey of the soul, that is, a spiritual participation in the world. The third round initiates are less focused on personal goals and are dedicated more to serving others. They are motivated by compassion to cultivate the well-being of others. The ultimate message is that the heroic image lies within, and that vicarious participation in myths enables individuals to come into contact with that image in themselves.

The four particular archetypes that I am investigating and using as categories to explore the mythic heroes are the shadow, anima, animus, and self. All archetypes have two sides to them, one constructive and the other destructive. One side brings light, the other darkness. One aspect is fertile, the other barren. So, when archetypes are active, people's responses to them will determine which side of the polarity will be unleashed into their lives. Hence, knowledge of the particular archetypes and the medium in which they express is helpful in the overall scheme of understanding people and their emotional states. Thus, the metaphysical pilgrims must make them conscious in a way that prevents them from exerting a harmful influence. Instead of husbands witnessing their wives as princesses one moment and as witches the next, they stop projecting the anima archetype onto real people. Instead, they recognize the feminine principle operating and heal the relationship with these real people. Thus, this insight brings about a transformation of consciousness. I am defining consciousness as the ability to receive and respond to a stimuli. Awareness is the key to receiving and responding with greater freedom. Moreover, this leads to further mobility within the psyche and to clearer decision making.

The shadow archetype is a powerful force in regards to the human creative capacity. When it is given an outlet for expression, it can aid in the development of many latent talents. When it is stifled, because people are unable to accept the chaotic component to themselves, it will unleash havoc onto an unsuspecting world. The animus is the masculine component in females and males. This is the part of women's psyches which seeks to express masculine attributes to help in balancing their lopsided psyches. It is the part of men's psyches which are usually well-developed given the reinforcing conditions of society. The anima is the feminine component to men's and women's psyches and functions much as does the animus, except it is the men's psyches which are lopsided and must be balanced. The self is the archetype which organizes and integrates the others. It brings ultimate stability to the psyche and leads it towards completeness.

Chapters four though seven consist of an analyses of four myths using the methodologies of Joseph Campbell and Carl Jung. These myths are in order of appearance *The Epic of Gilgamesh*, *Bhagavad Gita*, *Owein*, and *Star Wars*. I trace the roles of the protagonists in these myths through the three stages of the hero's journey developed by Campbell, namely, departure, initiation, and return, and then look at the four archetypes (shadow, animus, anima, and self) as to how they manifest in these myths. My basic objective is to show that there exist universal categories operating in mythic literature which reveal the journey towards psychic completeness. I am claiming that these categories are universal and appear not only in myths, but in the lives of all persons. Campbell believed that all lives are of mythic proportion. Generating within these lives are the impartial energies of the unconscious moving people to being wholly and completely integrated, thus psychically balanced. What occurs to heroic characters in myths literally happens in real life at a psychological level. People need to expand their awareness and recognize these mythic motifs, so that they can be heroes or heroines. This requires a great deal of inner courage, and willingness to be introspective, thus taking a sober look at the dark side of human nature. And making the decision to change the aspects of their personality which interfere with psychic development. For as long as the archetypes remain unconscious and consciousness does not perceive even the effects which they cause, they will elude being comprehended. Most people approach myths intellectually, which is fine in itself, but fail to utilize the potential in myths to facilitate personal growth. Human beings must move beyond knowing only the words, and learn to know the "substance of the thing from inside" (Jacobi 14). Myths must be participated in emotionally, wrenching all at the very center of being, causing participants to take a probing look at what arises.

Chapter Eight was a later development of my investigation into myths and the psyche. I call it "The Feminine Presence in Myths: An Ethical Imperative." I found a discussion of myths focusing on the journey of heroes without including heroines was as limited and lopsided as persons who had developed their animus to the exclusion of their anima. There seems to be a limited amount of mythic literature wherein females are protagonists, let alone the heroines. I believe the cause can be traced to the changes among paleolithic cultures. The roles of males and females shifted in these early agricultural, planting, gathering, and hunting cultures. A fear of the feminine developed within and amongst men, who learned to suppress the creative enterprises of women. These role changes became so reinforced and institutionalized, that what began as conscious suppression became unconscious repression. The men no longer remembered why they distrusted women. This repression led men to ignore the significance of women in literature. However, like all psychic elements, when repressed or denied, they surface in the most unusual of places. They cannot be hidden or forever erased from life. The psyche is whole from the beginning, and the parts which compose it are always and forever there. If any one of them could literally be removed or eliminated, then it all would collapse. The parts have no purposefulness without the whole and the whole cannot become complete without the parts. I subtitle the chapter "An Ethical Imperative" because, I believe in the utter necessity of materializing both the feminine and masculine principles into human awareness. When this critical event occurs, there will be, in addition to a transformation of consciousness, the possibility of a transformation of beingness. To speculate further, a real opportunity for morphological evolution. The biological transformation of the human organism, while quite fascinating, is not even the primary issue here. Ethically at stake is the survival of the human species. Cooperation amongst diverse peoples and their many ideologies is a necessary prerequisite for a harmoniously interacting global community. Integrating the attributes of the feminine psyche, while not reacting by then ignoring the masculine psyche, will lead to a more stable environment. This chapter, then, elaborates upon how this can be achieved and the consequences of such action.

The "Conclusion" shall be an interpretive summary to explain the outcome of my research and possible steps which may be taken to further investigation.

Before proceeding to Chapter One, I should like to discuss my use of "polar" terminology, and next to begin the understanding of myths by eliminating some of the common misconceptions surrounding them. The terms "masculine" and "feminine" are attached to numerous stereotypes in their association with men's and women's behavior. These stereotypes are socially accepted ways of perceiving gender differences. In reality, these "differences" are part of the psychological mindset of both men and women. With the exception of the biological differences (and these are not as great as many believe), there are no proven innate psychological differences. This is far from obvious when the words used to describe the genders can be quite one-sided. The term "compassion" for many denotes an image of a women, and "heroic" that of a man. And yet, I should consider Mother Teresa as heroic and Gandhi as being compassionate. Actually, they are both heroic and compassionate. And because Gandhi is kindhearted does not imply that he is effeminate anymore than Mother Teresa being rational and organized in creating her "Charities" is macho. My point is that all these various attributes of the personality whether dormant or not are within all bodies, regardless of their gender. It is because of social reinforcement that stereotypes arose and with them the terrible judgments that specific behaviors are "men only" and others "women only." So, when I use the terms "feminine principle" and "masculine principle," I shall be placing the emphasis on "principle." "Feminine" and "masculine" will be used to focus attention on the polar and complimentary nature of the archetypes. I encourage people to "unlearn" their associations of what they have been taught is manly or womanly behavior. They must follow the Tao of naturalness and relearn how to be true to their own natures. Myths tend to exaggerate and typecast their characters to make a point. Real life people are seldom so undeviating and definite in their actions. However, I shall elucidate on how, even in myths, the most successful and developed characters integrate masculine and feminine principles into their consciousnesses.

The term "myth" commonly means something that is false or not real. Everyone has heard people say: "That's just a myth," meaning it is not true. This is a misuse of the term, as myths never claimed to be about actual persons, or places, or events, although they can contain allusions to actual persons, places, or historical events. Myths often reveal truths without being "true" stories. When myths are viewed more as factual occurrences, people tend to become one-sided, closed-minded, and biased, because a challenge to literal interpretations can be viewed as a challenge to their belief systems. Joseph Campbell noted this phenomenon regarding the sacred literature of religion: When read literally, it often comes into conflict with science, reason, and common sense (*Open Life* 70). Some religious literature is historically accurate, although most of it was originally mythopoeic. Today the word "myth" frequently means a story about "supernatural incidents intended to explain nature, or one which deals with the gods and demons that were invented by early man" (Asimov 10). Asimov wrote:

> The Greeks took their myths seriously. Since the gods controlled natural forces, it was wise to treat them with careful consideration. They had to be bribed to send rain when it was needed, and pleaded with not to send disease or misfortune. For that reason, animals were sacrificed to them, beautiful temples were built for them, songs were composed to praise them. Thus, a religion grew up about the myths (*Ibid*).

Some other recent views about myths are that they "are stories about gods" (Gunkel xiv) and express "the early stage of [human beings'] intellectual development," with obscure events being attributed to intervening gods (Childs 13). Toppings wrote in the Introduction to *Bulfinch's Mythology*:

> Myths helped to explain the natural world. They were often grounded in physical reality, though their imagination reached far beyond the boundaries of empirical experience. Humans sought to explain themselves to themselves. Mythology was used to inspire the young and teach them while they were being entertained (6).

Likewise, Edith Hamilton agreed that myths are "an explanation of something in nature" (12). When there is a great storm at sea, it is Poseidon who is upset; a plague upon the land may mean that one of the gods has not been worshiped sufficiently. Thunder and lightning may have been attributed by the ancients to the gods, as they lacked a scientific explanation. Anthropomorphized natural phenomena may indeed be included in mythopoeic literature, but this is not mythology in and of itself.

Most of these explanations, thus far, discuss the content of myths. The content is a result of the psychodynamic processes at work within the unconscious mind. Therefore, myths are more than their content. They deal with processes that are given form and, when realized, add to the psychological and social well-being of people.

If people would regard myths more as they do fairy tales, as make-believe stories, then through their imagination, they would be able to derive from them the benefit that was intended. I realize that children regard fairy tales as real and, because they live them out in their imaginations, they are able to resolve conflicts within their psyches (Bettelheim 6). Likewise, when myths began to lose their association with ritual and were replaced by religious institutions, their effectiveness came into jeopardy (Campbell *Open Life* 69-70). Campbell stated that primitive cultures that have had their myths usurped by Western influence have become places of disease and vice. They have had their belief systems torn apart, and therefore, are left in a disarray of emotional wandering. When people understand that myths do not represent answers but "are attempts to express insights" (*Ibid* 23) about human nature, they derive a greater benefit from reading them. Bettelheim, in referring to children's literature, and I think myths fit his statement too, said that they become "devalued when what people have learned to read adds nothing of importance to their lives" (4).

In addition to Campbell, Frazer referred to myths in *The Golden Bough* as reenacting ritual. Eliade made similar claims regarding creation myths in that a particular place and time became sacred because the participants in myths were ritually repeating the way the world was "when the Divine Being was on earth" (*Rites & Symbols* 7). Beane wrote about Eliade's ideas that every ritual has an archetypal model (133). Thus, it aids in the return to the original moment which precedes the creation of time and space. Rituals are the acting out of symbols and "they function to make concrete and experimental the mythic values of a society" (*Ibid* 164). Some persons fail to experience this process today because they have bracketed out ritual and have lost themselves in mundane activities. Campbell vividly details a story about aboriginal circumcision initiations and wrote that in primal initiation rites the boy "has been removed from his childhood, and his body has been scarified. Now he has a man's body. There's no chance of relapsing back to boyhood after a show like that" (*Power of*

Myth 82). Boys and girls today have few chances of enacting myths leading to much needed psychological transformations (*Ibid*).

W. Robertson Smith in his *Lectures on the Religion of the Semites* (1889) introduced his theory of sacrifice as being a communion which the human being "shares in the vital force of the consumed animal;" thus, "the sacrificial animal is raised to divine status, so that myths arise from a social rite" (Edmunds 29). Jane Harrison viewed myths as being created in order to explain rites (Edmunds 31), that is, as a reflection of social events, such as initiations. And in one other view that they arise together: myths are the *legomenon*, the bring spoken, and the rituals are the *drömenon*, the thing done. Myths are part of the dramatic ritual (Edmunds 33). And C. Kluckhohn in his "Myths and Rituals: A General Theory" writes that "people cannot speak of priority in the relation between myths and rituals: "Myths are a system of object and act symbols" (Edmunds 40). E. Leach said that "myths are the counterpart of rituals: myths imply rituals, rituals imply myths; they are one and the same (Edmunds 40).

Myths and rituals seem to be different aspects of the same underlying psychological substratum. Rituals are the dances of myths. There are different rituals performed reflective of the mythic motif at hand, just as there are different dances done bringing to life various stories. It appears relevant to discuss myths and rituals as belonging together, with neither one preceding the other. People who act in certain ways may be doing so as the result of archetypal influences and thus in the act be reflecting unconsciously generated mythic motifs. When myths are told to people, the listeners of those tales, now participants, give them life. Myths only have life to the degree individuals respond to them at a "gut" level. An act that is not produced by archetypal forces is not a ritual; it lacks mythic elements and thus is an empty dance—one without purposefulness. Modern day television is an empty dance which momentarily entertains without having a transformative affect on viewers.

Myths, to be powerful, must be part of rituals, even if those rituals are not very overt. And rituals must be the dances that draw upon the psyche's energy or they are no more than thoughtless routines. Myths may be created, but they are not myths until they are given life (ritualized). People may go through the actions of various rituals, but those rituals are dead until they are connected to what is mythic. They cannot exist apart from the other. They must each represent the dynamic interplay of the psyche's subterranean processes, speaking and dancing to the voices of the archetypes. The myths that I will analyze are alive because they still affect the hearers or viewers of them, today. They stimulate emotional and cognitive changes in the participants who vicariously ritualize the experiences.

Chapter One

The Symbol's Journey: Archetypal Expression

Myths communicate to human beings using the language of symbols and metaphors, words which release power and prepare people for meaning. This language arises in response to the unrelenting demand from the unconscious to find an outlet for its energies, namely, the archetypes. Archetypes are of a transcendent nature, and any attempt to describe them conceptually leads to paradox. Thus, reality is masked in the language of symbols, which myths attempt to unmask by translating the images projected from the archetypes of the unconscious to consciousness. In order to understand and appreciate this function of myths, people need to know something about the human psyche and the way it functions.

According to Carl Jung, the psyche is divided into the unconscious and consciousness. Jung uses the term "psyche" to refer to both the unconscious and consciousness, whereas "mind" is avoided as it is typically associated with consciousness. The unconscious is further divided into the personal unconscious, which consists of people's acquired and then stored experiences, and the collective unconscious, which is innate and universal and constitutes a "common psychic substrate of a suprapersonal nature which is present in everyone" (Jung *CW* 9:1, 4). The collective unconscious is an impersonal, objective phenomena (*CW* 9:1, 22) which does not reason. This unconscious is in reality a "no-thing," that is, it is not a "thing," but a process for releasing potential. The deeds that people do, the thoughts they think, their fates (*CW* 9:1, 279), their destinies, lie in slumber in this fathomless chamber of the psyche, awakening at the proper moment, impacting with their conscious experiences, to make them who and what they are. Jung wrote that "just as the human body is a museum, so to speak, of its phylogenetic history, so too is the psyche" (*CW* 9:1, 287).

Contained in the collective unconscious are the archetypes, Jung wrote about the term "archetype" being derived from the Greek *archetupos*, which originated with Philo Judaeus in regards to the "*Imago Dei*" (God-images) in human beings; Irenaeus stated that "the creator of the world did not fashion these things directly from himself but copied them from archetypes outside himself"; the *Corpus Hermeticum* calls God the "archetypal light;" the terms "immaterial Archetypes" and "Archetypal stone" are mentioned in Dionysius the Areopagite; Augustine wrote of the unformed "*ideae principales*" contained in God's mind; Levy-Bruhl referred to the symbolic images of primitives as "répresentations collectives" (*CW* 9:1, 4-5). Thus "archetype" and its associated concepts have been in use for a long time.

Arche (Greek) means "beginning," and type from *tupos* (Greek) means "impress," "imprint," "pattern" (Johnson *Inner Work* 29) or "blow." Thus archetype means the "prime imprinter," that is, the most basic model. Jung used "primordial image," "inherited pathways," and "deposits" before putting into use the term "archetype." He stopped using these terms because he realized that they implied something evolving through repetition (Bidney 17). It is the human organism that evolves to become in the image of the archetypes. The archetypes do not evolve, but do take varying shapes in the content of people's dreams, myths, and imaginations. As people change, so do their archetypal images. The archetypes behind the images remain the same. The images become shapeshifters to meet the needs of individuals. To be more specific, the archetypes, themselves, are energies stored in the collective unconscious with the potential for "imagizing." They are "patterns of psychic energy, of life energy, much as the structure of the universe consists of energies" (Harding *I & Not-I* 136) that find expression in matter. What undergoes repetition and change are not the archetypes but the behavioral responses to them. This is similar to saying that gravity does not evolve, as it operates according to specific laws of nature. The principle by which gravity affects masses is the same. However, as masses vary in size, gravity will affect them according to their own nature. Gravity is not altered by this interaction. Archetypes, I believe, function in a like manner. Archetypal energies are active, and yet are latent, lying in wait for the right stimulus from the environment to release them in what becomes an ongoing dance with matter. I tend to believe these archetypal energies are being driven by the "Creator's" Image, That which imagines the cosmos. This Image uses the archetypal energies to "learn" from their experiences with matter, as to what combinations work best to actualize life to be "in the image and likeness of . . ." These energies are learning better ways of interacting with matter as the result of the age-long experiences of life that all creatures have passed through. This formless Image works through the energies of archetypes, and becomes something concrete, with shape or form when integrated with matter.

This is Jung's greatest contribution to the reshaping of psychoanalysis, his concept of the collective unconscious and its archetypes. He rooted the psyche into the cosmos. The archetypes being the seeds from which life grows. He moved the psyche from a strictly biological dimension to a cosmological dimension. He evolved the concept of what it is to be human from a child of the earth to also one of the stars.

Before writing further on the archetypes, I feel that I must elaborate on the concept of the collective unconscious. It is the field for the interplaying of psychic energies, in a similar way the galaxies and universe is the space in which the physical energies or forces (strong, weak, electro-magnetic, gravitational) participate. These energies exist in all forms of life. It is only when they operate through self-conscious beings that they can be directed. A lightbulb has form but no power until electricity combines with it. The electricity has power but no way to materialize until it unites with a form. Energy without matter has no expression; matter without energy has no life. It is within the time-space dimension that they join for the cosmic dance. Thus, it would make sense that the archetypal energies exist prior to the time-space dimension, but have manifestation in it. If these energies are dependent on the time-space continuum, then they must change and evolve with it. Preceding it, they can participate in it while remaining unscathed.

Life exists as a great cosmic web of interacting energies. These energies are formless without their counterpart matter. And matter is lifeless without these energies. The dualistic worldview of Cartesian philosophy is no longer realistic in light of the discoveries in subatomic physics. Add to this the agelong claims of mystics, with their unifying views of cosmic reality, and the evidence begins to mount. For discussion's sake, analyzing the whole in terms of its parts can shed light on how it works. Then, to believe that the parts are separate from the whole, that is, can exist without interacting with each other, is a critical error in judgment. Everything in the universe sustains everything. If space is removed, then there is no place for form. It is senseless to discuss the one without simultaneously recognizing the essentialness of the other. And in reality, the one is the other and the other is the one. They are actually only different manifestations of each other; degrees of the same thing; variations in potential.

Archetypes and instincts are unconscious movers that stimulate consciousness into an orderly existence. In addition, the archetypes have another side to them, that of a "spiritual model" somewhat analogous to Plato's ideal forms or *eidos* which are preexisting patterns in the celestial sphere. Plato's forms are a "philosophical expression of the psychological archetypes" and lack the dynamism and generative force of the archetypes (Jacobi 49-50). Archetypes are similar to Platonic forms in that they are projected into the world presenting the human "soul" with the opportunity to climb the spiritual ladder to "heaven." This is the unification of unconscious with consciousness; Jung's process of individuation. Individuation is another important extension of psychoanalysis in that it appeals to the self-actualizing urges in people. It removes humans from being the pawn of irrational, instinctive forces and places them as the guardians and transformers of their destinies.

Archetypes may be represented by mythic images, but are themselves formless. Archetypes store the memories of human ancestry, not of individual persons, but of the experiences of the species. A further movement in psychoanalysis in seen by Jung taking into account the group mind or world soul, the emotional impressions of humankind, not only those from personal biographies. Ken Wilber writes that creation is patterned after the archetypes (*Eye* 242) and that the collective unconscious contains the collective motifs of the human race: "All the gods and goddesses, divinities and demons, heroes and villains portrayed outwardly by the world's ancient mythologies are contained, in condensed form, in the depths of human beings". Though people may be unaware of it, "according to Jung, archetypes live on and continue to move people deeply in ways both creative and destructive" (Wilber *No Boundary* 126). Archetypes are analogous to the biological instincts, yet, they are not "vague and indefinite by nature, but are specifically formed motive forces which pursue their inherent goals" regardless of the presence of consciousness (Jung *CW* 9:1, 43). Jung felt that the archetypes are the "unconscious images of the instincts" (*CW* 9:1, 44). I should interpret that to mean that archetypes are the psychological energies behind what is carried out biologically by the instincts. When two seeds fall to the ground, one is in darkness and dies, one is in light and lives. Something made the seed move toward the light—told it that this was the right direction to follow (not to be repelled by but attracted to light). After much repetition, all plants would now "instinctively" seek out light. This desire or capacity was inborn, innate within the plant. This is the inherent program in the plant's "psyche" which interacts with the material world finding expression. Likewise, archetypes move human beings in their behavior. Archetypes are like genes, in that as genes influence physical traits, likewise do archetypes affect psychic life, which in turn affects behavior. These changes in behavior can stimulate dormant archetypes, as they need an outer object to be projected onto in order to manifest themselves in consciousness.

Archetypes produce symbols, images and ideas which find expression in all human beings as variations of a timeless motif. These archetypal images are affected by people's environments, experiences, and social structures. Archetypes are predispositions or tendencies for behavior which have existed since the beginning. They are the cosmic energies everready to be actualized in living tissue. They are the result of unconscious processes that acquire shape when they become conscious and are perceived. Finally, taking their color from the consciousness with which they are interacting (Jung *CW* 9:1, 5).

People become aware of archetypes as they are projected onto the world and are made known to them through their thoughts, feelings, and actions. External reality is the mirror which reflects the processes of the unconscious. The external world acts as the playground for the archetypes (the script), and the psyche is both their director (unconscious) and audience (consciousness). Making friends with the archetypes by recognizing patterns of behavior helpful to individuals and eliminating behavior which conflicts with them leads people towards healthy-mindedness and away from psychological "dis-ease" (meaning lack of homeostasis).

Just as physicists have realized that observation alters the behavior of subatomic particles, likewise, is this true of the psyche, that the archetypes' symbols are changed following the archetypes entrance into consciousness. The uncertainty principle operates in the psyche in that the observers interfere with what is being observed. Language, being part of the conceptual mode of understanding, creates dualism when it attempts to explain a process which cannot be placed exclusively at either end of a pole.

As I wrote in my openings comments, the unconscious speaks to humankind in images that are translated into words, which are devices to label, analyze, and give structure to the energies which arise out of the collective unconscious. New words or word pictures, that is, symbols, are invented to make sense of these universal expressions of energy which filter through individual and communal consciousnesses. Symbols provide objectivity to the profundity of human thought. They "are metaphors for the eternal in the forms of the transient; in them the two are 'thrown together,' fused into a unity of meaning" (Jacobi 77).

The numerous environments in which cultures arise create a need for new images to which words are then attached. Language, as such, does not generate new images, but transforms people's ways of thinking about them. Therefore, a society which lives in an environment of snow and ice will use snow and ice as part of its mythic images. Another society which has its culture unfold in a desert, though their images will be different, can certainly tell the same story as the nomads of the ice culture. The content of myths are not ultimately relevant for understanding mythology as a whole but only for individual interpretations of myths and to that to which it points. The symbols and metaphors that are building blocks of myths may wear different masks as they impact with different cultures, but do not change in essential meaning. What changes is the way these images are able to help transform the consciousnesses of those who use them.

When a culture changes radically, the traditional symbol may be replaced by a new one which is recognized as being more meaningful. The other change is when the traditional symbol has been integrated into a people's psyche to the extent that they have transcended the need for those particular symbols. For example, some people might come to regard the cross upon which Jesus was crucified as symbolic of the good and evil natures of human beings. On one side of Jesus was a thief who refused to acknowledge God and ask for forgiveness. This thief represents the negative pole of human nature. On the other side of Jesus was a thief who repented and was forgiven. He was told that he would join Jesus in heaven. This other thief represents the positive pole of human nature. Jesus died on the arms of the cross, which represent the horizontal, time-space dimension of life. However, he transcended this world of duality, and hence defeated death, by identifying with the Father, the vertical dimension of the cross. In this tale of the two thieves, there is both a literal and symbolic dimension. As will be shown, Joseph Campbell taught mostly about the symbolic interpretation of such stories. He might interpret it as symbolic of humankind's own psychic and spiritual shortcomings which can be transcended. The symbol of the cross becomes for such persons a catalyst for inner transformation. As long as symbols remain facts, human growth will be limited and unidimensional. A balance needs to occur between the tunnel vision of single-mindedness and the peripheral vision of open-mindedness, so that the focus may be maintained when contemplating symbols. Eventually the outward gaze will be turned inward until the symbol disappears altogether and is replaced by the personal experience.

Grappling with psychological explanation leads to the formation of new myths, as this process is but translating symbols into newer, better suited ones (Jacobi 118). When the body is punctured, it immediately begins to fill that hole. The unconscious, likewise, fills the psychological holes caused by failure to integrate successfully the archetypal energies into consciousness. If voids remain in people, new symbols and myths will be generated to fill them. Symbols are not consciously generated, but are "spontaneous products of unconscious psychic activity" (Jacobi 105). It is the patterns and the psychic processes behind these patterns of psychic activity that are universal and collective in their nature. Hence, a psychological understanding of the myths enables people to become aware of the ceaseless process behind the forms. Physicists have discovered that the physical form is composed of electrons in perpetual motion, and it is their aggregation that causes the appearance of a solid mass.

Words, the instruments of thought, do not alter the archetypes, but allow them to be approached from a multitude of perspectives. Thus people are able to make sense of them in a personal way. Ultimately, the many paths that are tread lead to the same place, and when that place is reached, people will realize that there are no more pathseekers or places to be sought. This is the transcendent nature of the collective unconscious.

Symbols are not about the objective world, although they are represented by objects. Experiences trigger the construction of symbols and, when they are participated in and reasoned upon, they clarify these experiences. Symbols have the "capacity for expressing paradoxical situations or certain patterns of ultimate reality that can be expressed in no other way" (Beane 349). Symbols are a step towards familiarity with the ultimate ground of Reality and thus manifest the universal in the personal experiences of people.

Symbols speak directly to people and arouse their emotional sensitivities. Emotions are not aroused by stimulating the rational faculties but by the stimulation of unconscious elements (Middleton 79). In a sense a "spark is struck forth, for emotion is the chief source of consciousness. There is no change from darkness to light or from inertia to movement without emotion" (Jung *CW* 9:1, 96).

Jung went so far as to write: "Emotion is not an activity of individuals but something that happens to them. Affects usually occur where adaptation is weakest" (*CW* 9:2, 9). The weakness is due to a lack of consciousness integrating archetypal motifs. Johnson writes that the "unconscious invades conscious minds and attempts to express itself—through the *imagination*, using the symbolic language of feeling-charged images" (*Inner Work* 2). Furthermore, Johnson contends that Jung clearly demonstrated that the unconscious functions as the creative source of all that evolves into consciousness and into the human personality (*Ibid* 6). Thus, it is important to read the symbol correctly to understand better people's personalities.

Freud and Jung disagreed on the importance and function of symbols. Freud thought them to be another reference for something that was already known. For instance, a stop sign means to stop and nothing more. Jung, on the other hand, interpreted symbols as pointing to that which is as yet unknown (Frey-Rohn 261). The collective unconscious used recognizable images in the form of symbols to awaken consciousness to something unknown. The message is hidden in the symbol. Therefore, a stop sign does not mean to stop but refers to something unknown by consciousness.

Symbols are also the language of rites and rituals, and when acted out provide more emotional intensity and power to persuade. Symbols can arise spontaneously from within the psyche or as logical constructs which are derived associations between the perceivers and their environments. An animal which is observed acting with strength, speed, and cunning may turn into a symbol of what is admired in human beings. Symbols can have a plurality of meanings, whereas signs have but one (Beane 342). A stop sign means to stop, nothing else. Signs can easily be replaced or changed, whereas a symbol touches on the essence of the human condition, and is not readily changed as it points to that which is unchangeable and which is beyond itself. Symbols arise spontaneously, not being rationally contrived or invented. In referring to Jung's ideas, Kolokithas writes:

> Although part of the fabric of the past, symbols are essentially future-oriented. They invite people to 'dream the myth onwards.' While rational consciousness thinks in terms of days and weeks, the unconscious thinks in terms of millennia. The more people learn to understand symbols, the more 'the energy that belongs to them can flow freely into humankind.' When persons read symbols 'correctly,'
> they transform themselves. This transforms the species as a whole, balancing one-sided rational consciousness with the life-force of universal mind (12).

Jung wrote that "there are as many archetypes as there are typical situations in life. Endless repetition has engraved these experiences into humankind's psychic constitution, not in the form of images filled with content, but at first only as forms without content, representing merely the possibility of a certain type of perception and action" (*CW* 9:1, 48). People's experiences activate certain archetypes, causing them to appear compulsive in their behavior, much in the way an instinct gains influence over reason and will. As archetypes form the oldest layer of the psyche, they consist of "psychic processes and functions that were active long before rational consciousness emerged." (Kolokithas 10). This is why it is necessary to recognize what the various archetypes are and how they function in people's lives. To comment on Jung's belief that there are many archetypes, I believe that at the essential level there is only the archetypal process. The archetypes are but potentials for behavior and action. There is only one energy in the cosmos. Though there are many ways this energy may express, through many forms. All forms have their own specific "activity pattern," that, I am saying is the same energy in different patterns. To write of unlimited archetypes, as many archetypes as there are situations, is to mean unlimited possibilities for energy to manifest and express itself.

Thus, as part of my methodological lens, I shall discuss and describe the four primary archetypes which occur throughout the myths being investigated. These archetypes include the shadow, anima, animus, and self. The shadow represents those elements within the psyche that are contrary to people's conscious attitudes and, hence, are denied. This refusal to acknowledge this dark side of human character results in a "split" personality. The shadow is "dark" only because it is the opposite of what people consciously and socially think is right and, not because it in itself is evil or wrong. Shadow elements which are denied are projected onto the world and viewed by consciousness as darkness and demons. A watchful eye must be kept on the shadow so that people do not act destructively toward society. Hitler projected his shadow onto the world, rather than to acknowledge the conflict of psychic forces at play within himself, resulting in the loss of much human life. The shadow shows individuals their weaknesses and all the things they do not like about themselves. It is also the primeval part of the psyche and thus supplies people with many of their natural instincts and creative tendencies. Therefore, the shadow needs to be integrated into conscious life so that people can use its vital energies to maintain contact with their emotions and spontaneity. A sudden outburst of rage is the release of the instinctual energy of the shadow. Being alarmed at this disparate fit of temper leaves people mulling, "I don't know what came over me," or "I'm not quite myself today." This occurs when the shadow elements come into conflict with social and personal standards. However, the sudden outburst of creativity that results in writing a poem or painting a picture can also be a byproduct of the shadow.

The anima is the feminine principle in the male's psyche. The animus is the masculine principle in the female's psyche. Jungians do not usually speak of a man as having an animus or a woman as having an anima, because biological and social conditions have seen to it that men are male and women are female, naturally. Although, I find it helpful to acknowledge the anima and animus as functioning in both men and women. This is similar to how a Taoist might view *yin* and *yang* as functioning in both genders. Perhaps it might be "more" Jungian to state that there is a "masculine" and "feminine" principle operating in both sexes. I should like to remain open to the notion that anima and animus operate in both men and women, keeping in mind that this is not, at present, the most common way of discussing them. Afterall, a man who does not feel comfortable with his masculinity might discard that part, tossing it into the shadow. Or he might project overly masculine qualities through his persona, the social mask he wears, in order to protect himself from what might be a painful discovery, that he prefers being effeminate. With such persons, it might be useful to further the healing process by discussing their concepts of what is animus or masculine about men, and vice versa for women.

The anima and animus are based on psychological principles and not social notions of femaleness or maleness. It is biology that determines the role of the anima or animus in the human psyche. The feminine principle is found in symbols such as the god Dionysus, intuition, the goddess Aphrodite, the moon, and passivity. The anima deals mostly with the inner world. Some symbols of the masculine principle are the god Apollo, knowledge, the warrior, the hero, the sun, and activity. The animus focuses primarily on the outer world. The anima makes peace, the animus conquers. This is why a docile woman may fall in love with a strong, robust man and he, in turn, may fall in love with a quiet, gentle woman. Each personifies to the other those qualities within themselves that are in need of conscious development. Each projects the latent best that is within their psyches onto others and falls in love with those projected images. What people need to do is to integrate those projected qualities into themselves to become more complete. Once the projecting onto others falls away, the lovers may or may not like what they see. For then they are seeing these others in their nakedness, without the veil of projected psychic elements covering their "love" objects.

The self archetype is the most important as far as being the one which draws together all the other archetypes. It seeks to bring about order and balance. It is symbolized by the square, circle, mandala, wise old man or woman, and God. The self is the ordering element of both the unconscious and consciousness. The self is wholeness, not of parts being put together, for it is already total. It involves a maturing of people's psychological natures. When people feel at peace with the world, sensing harmony and oneness, this is the work of the self. The self is the inner light and the inner guide which awakens individuals to who they are and to what they are becoming.

Chapter Two

The Symbol's Appearance: Mythography

In Chapter One I introduced the readers to how in Jungian theory the archetypes find expression through symbols. One of the chief ways in which archetypes come to symbolic expression is in myths. I shall now briefly describe the nature of myths, focusing particularly on how they are linked to the psychic dimension of human beings. I shall present an overview of some of the chief interpreters of myths in use today and their ideas about them. I do not intend to exhaust the interpretative categories; rather, I shall briefly survey what I believe to be the most useful views in regards to the development of human beings. The psychological schools of thought, specifically those of Carl Jung and Joseph Campbell, will be my primary focus. Their methodologies will also be used to analyze the myths found in chapters Four through Seven, as I believe they are best suited for understanding and proliferating psychic integration.

The term "myth" is derived from the Greek *muthos*, meaning "word" or "speech." It is "the word for a story concerning gods and superhuman beings" (Bolle 261). Myths connect people to the sacred—the ground of being. They connect humans with their primordial processes from which human psychic life developed. Myths do no seek to inspire argumentation or analysis of a subject; rather, they intend to present the subject as "the way it is." Myths are the voices of human origins, presenting and taking Homo sapiens to creation, not debating it (Bolle 262). Myths infuse the world with transcendent images to which people could not readily relate without the language of symbols. And the task of deciphering symbols can be quite formidable. Myths speak with the voice of authority, because they reveal fundamental truths about human nature.

Greeks such as Pythagoras and Thales regarded myths, for example those found in the *Iliad*, as allegories of nature. As allegories, they are not peopled with real beings, but "personifications of natural phenomena or poetic designations for the elements" (Patai 11), thus signifying the emotional struggle within all persons. Another view, developed by Xenophanes about 600 B.C.E., tried to explain them rationally. His famous statement is:

> Mortals suppose that the gods are born, and that they wear human clothing and have human voices and bodies but if cattle or lions had hands, so as to paint with their hands and produce works of art as humans do, they would paint their gods and give them bodies in form like their own, horses like horses, cattle like cattle (Bolle 268).

The Sophists and later the Neoplatonic and Stoic philosophers saw myths as exploring moral truths and principles, where the gods were equated with the elements or moral qualities (Patai 11-12).

Euhemerus of the third century B.C.E. began a rational inquiry into the beings of mythology. Euhemerus recounted a tale about the island of Parchaia where he came across a temple of Zeus. He inferred that an historical figure by the name of Zeus had once erected a haven there and then later died in Crete. In this way he reduced Zeus from a god to a great leader. Hecataeus of Teos, who lived in Egypt around 323 B.C.E., tried to explain the gods as glorified human benefactors (Geffcken 572-73).

The Judeo-Christian tradition with its emphasis on monotheism viewed the gods of the pagans as simply mortals. These pagan gods, reduced to being mere mortals, were intermingled with personalities from the Old Testament (Patai 13-14), and found their way into Renaissance art, as for example, on the Sistine Ceiling. Bidney wrote of Vico (1668-1744) that he "appreciated the ethnological value of myths as containing significant historic records of the cyclical evolution of human thought and social institutions," as well their being accurate narratives of historical events (2). Friedrich Schleiermacher (1768-1834) believed the mythical to be a "historical representation of the supra-historical" because myths were not subject to history, but expressed in it (Bolle 269). Voltaire (1694-1778), a proponent of the rational school of thought, tried to reduce myths, as well as the Bible, to superstition or fiction conjured by deceptive priests to sway and control the masses.

Joseph Fontenrose's conception of the term "myth" was used indiscriminately as it was grouped with ritual, belief, magic, and theology. He felt myth should mean what it traditionally has meant: stories about gods, spirits, and supernatural beings that are orally transmitted narratives, and considered to be real stories about events which occurred in the distant past (54). Fontenrose made some important statements about how myths are modified to meet institutional and political changes in a society (58). A prime example is how Aeschylus's (525-456 B.C.E.) *Eumenides* introduced "extenuating circumstances" or the "motive" into his story as a way of protesting the Athenian judicial system's treatment of murder cases. The myth and ritual school had its day with such proponents as Jane E. Harrison (*Themis*) and S. H. Hooke, who believed that myths grow out of rites and that the spoken work took on the power of an act (Patai 25). Over a period of time what was said and done lost its correlative power and the word was opened to diverse literary and artistic formations (*Ibid* 26). Patai noted that perhaps the most significant single conclusion that can be drawn from this "profusion of studies in the field of myth criticism is that the twentieth century is as much a mythopoeic age as was the period of Homer in ancient Greece nearly three thousand years ago" (44).

Bidney asserted that Ernst Cassirer (1874-1945) also attempted to systematize myth and culture referring to Cassirer's ideas that "mythical thinking is a unitary form of consciousness. There are no unity of objects in myths but only a unity of functions expressed in a unique mode of experiences" (3). Myths are the voices of consciousness revealing a spiritual reality. Words in myths become powerful revealers of primal reality. Cassirer believed that, in myths, the fundamental human experience of the universe and its enunciation are inseparable. The differences between subject and object are nullified (Doty 175).

G. S. Kirk does not believe that myths "have a single form, or act according to one simple set of rules" (2). "There is no one definition of myths, no Platonic form of myths against which all actual instances can be measured. Myths differ enormously in their morphology and their social function" (*Ibid* 7), and are more than tales about gods. For example, Oedipus is a human being who does his best to disprove and avoid the fate prophesied by the oracle. Gilgamesh, although two-thirds a god, is treated as a human king and does not achieve physical immortality. Gods and fate play a role in these stories; yet, the story line does not revolve around them, but around the lives of their human characters. The characters in the *Iliad* undergo emotionally and physically arduous adventures, and Achilleus transforms his character. This hero's strength comes from within himself, not from the gods, nor from his relationship to the gods. This supports Kirk's thesis that myths are more than tales about gods. Caldwell divides Kirk's ideas about myth into three functions: "narrative and entertaining: operative and validatory (ritual and religion); and speculative and explanatory (myths that reflect or explain fundamental paradoxes or institutions)." Caldwell further notes that Kirk suggested a subjective function of myths with their use of symbols and fantasies (5). However, Kirk does not examine myths in the light of depth psychology or psychoanalysis, for that matter. A typology, to be more useful, needs to incorporate the psychological dimension from which all other readings of myths are born.

The structuralist approach of French anthropologist Claude Lévi-Strauss stated that myths are a form of communication, like music. It is the structure behind the sounds (music) or behind the words (myth) and their relationship to each other that is important. Myths are narratives that reflect different views: cosmological, sociological. No one view is the correct one by itself. Like music, myths have many parts that blend together to make a whole. As found in Morford, Lévi-Strauss insists that "all human behavior is based on certain unchanging patterns whose structure is the same in all ages and in all societies." Myths are the result of the binary structure of the mind which mediates between the polarities which develop, such as good/evil, love/hate. Thus myths seek to reveal opposites and resolve them (6). Therefore, the messages in myths are conveyed by their structures and relationships. Lévi-Strauss wrote "Du Miel aux cendres" in volume II of *Mythologiques*, page 407, as quoted by Kirk: "Non plus par réference á une réalité externe, mais selon les affinitiés ou les incompatibilités qu'ils manifestent les uns vis-á-vis des autres dans l'architecture de l'esprit" (45). According to Kirk, Lévi-Strauss thinks of l'esprit as a "structure of the human mind, which is the same all over the world" and works according to a process of binary analysis (45). Myths help to clarify the binary component of the mind in a way which is socially and intellectually comprehensible. The different contents of myths signify something because of their relationship to each other (Edmunds 343). In most cases the mind creates, compares, and makes resolutions between opposites. There are intuitive, transcendental, and mystical states that move beyond binary resolution and are not accounted for as to their influence on myths. Structuralists seek to find meaning in what generates myths by isolating "patterns of similarity and repetition that cut across the temporal narrative sequence" (Edmunds 367). Lévi-Strauss does not account for the importance of unrelated elements that often prove to be of value (Edmunds 367-8).

Bronislav Malinowski asserts that:

> Studied alive, myths are not an explanation in satisfaction of a scientific interest, but a narrative resurrection of a primeval reality, told in satisfaction of deep religious wants, moral cravings, social submissions, assertions, even practical requirements. Myths fulfill an indispensable function: they express, enhance, and codify belief; they safeguard and enforce morality; they vouch for the efficiency of ritual and contain practical rules for the guidance of humans. Myths are thus a vital ingredient of human civilisations; they are not idle tales, but hard-worked active forces; they are not intellectual explanations or artistic imageries, but pragmatic charters of primitive faith and moral wisdom. These stories are to the natives a statement of a primeval, greater, and more relevant reality, by which the present life, fates and activities of humankind are determined, the knowledge of which supplies humans

with the motive for ritual and moral actions, as well as with indications as to how to perform them (101, 108).

Malinowski believed that myths are intimately connected with social institutions. And though this is useful, he does not account satisfactorily for the dynamism of the human psyche and its influence on cultural constructs.

Thus far, I have written about various perspectives on what myths are. The next step is to look at what myths do, that is, their function for those who are listeners or observers of myths and for those who are the performers in the rituals associated with those myths. Let me point out that the aforementioned theories on myths regard them as tales about nature, reflections of the elements, moral principles, anthropomorphisms, exaggerations of human abilities, records of history and society, supernatural beings, mere fictions, and processes of the unconscious. All of these explanations have an element of truth in them, but with the exception of the psychological, lack pragmatic value in as far as they do not contribute to an understanding of the transformative nature of myths.

Joseph Campbell wrote about myths having four functions. The first is the mystical function which calls upon the adventurers to "waken and maintain an experience of awe, in recognition of that ultimate mystery, transcending names and forms" (*Creative* 609); and to reconcile "waking consciousness to the *mysterium tremendum et fascinans* of this universe *as it is*" (*Creative* 4). This opening allows these travelers to view the world from within, and to walk with more confidence upon the ultimate ground of all being, what is commonly referred to as God. It is this mystical view that relates people to the many manifestations of life to realize its harmony.

Eliade's concept of myths is supportive of Campbell's mystical function. Eliade believed that myths act as models for those events significant to human beings, such as marriage, art and education. Myths are regarded by the initiated as true stories. What they tell took place during sacred time and, as this inspires a sense of awe, are viewed as real. Secular stories are told to anyone anywhere and at anytime. These mythic tales recount events that took place in the distant past and are not common to everyday experiences. They do not relate stories about changes in human events, but tell of possible changes in the "human condition." Eliade felt that myths were cosmogonic and told of the growth of the human character (*Myth & Reality* 8-11), thus supplying persons with their existential groundings. It was this cosmological dimension of myths that Jung was especially attracted to and which contributed to his moving away from Freud's personalistic viewing of them.

Moreover, Campbell wrote that the second function of myths is the cosmological, which allows people to perceive the outer world as a whole. Campbell referred to the ideas of the nineteenth century ethnologist Adolf Bastian, as he found them useful to further illustrate Jung's concept of the archetype. Bastian wrote of *Elementargedanken* (elementary ideas) which reflect universal motifs common to all human beings and of *Völkergedanken* (ethnic ideas) which refers to a specific culture and locale, and how both are expressed in myths. The elementary ideas were explained through the ethnic ideas which provided the images of their specific environment. This cosmological function explains why myths often appear to be quite different, but are essentially the same. They are dressed in different style clothes, but what lies under their garments is the same (*Primitive* 461-62).

Campbell's third function of myths is sociological: "the enforcement of a moral order: the shaping of individuals to the requirements of their geographically and historically conditioned social group" (*Creative* 4-5). Myths bind people to their group and send the message that their way of life is valid and supported by the group.

This social function of myths is often fulfilled when it is used within religious rituals. Here the myths serve to "maintain the memory of, and provide authority for trivial customs and institutions" (Kirk 256). Tribal customs, ceremonial objects, and perfunctory places "are accepted because their genealogy can be stated; they are related to the mythical time when everything was placed in order and achieved once and for all its proper nature" (*Ibid* 257). They are "rarely just wish-fulfillment, and the primary myth-makers may be said to stand closer to reality than do the philosophers who use myths as second-best" (*Ibid* 259).

In a section of his *Völkerpsychologie* entitled "Mythus und Kultus," Wilhelm Wundt wrote about nature myths, implying that the believability of myths is due to the ritualized acts which represent the manifestation of emotional awe. Ritual elicits aid from the gods and is as well a form of supplication to them (23-24). People living today may say that their life is the way it is because a certain number of events occurred. An historian might tell them that their life is the result of much earlier events: the rise of agricultural communities, development of the Roman legal system, Protestant revolution, Newtonian physics, and more. People of long ago made claims and attributed their existence to events controlled by supernatural beings, occurring in a mythical past. Although they may have been unaware of the historicity of events perceived as causal agents in ritual. Most people today follow a linear path in regards to the irreversibility of past events; their ancestors recycled these events, keeping them alive (Eliade *Myth & Reality* 12-13).

The fourth function of myths, according to Campbell, is psychological and of primary importance as it is the foundation upon which the other three functions rest. This function acts as a teacher and guide for humankind through their journey from childhood on (*Animal Power* I, 9). Campbell said that this function serves "to foster the centering and unfolding of individuals in integrity, in accord with themselves (the microcosm), their culture (the mesocosm), the universe (the macrocosm), and that awesome ultimate mystery which is both beyond and within themselves and all things" (*Creative* 6).

Some discussion of the psychoanalytic school is necessary because it provided the impetus to the initial development of Jung's theories on the psyche and myths. In addition to this, it is a valid interpretive theory for the study of myths. Caldwell writes in his preface to *The Origin of the Gods* that myths are multi-functional. The psychological function is present in all myths. It has a three-foal goal: to let the unconscious express itself; to change the emotion of myths; and to supply society with a response to its psychological needs (ix). Likewise,

Caldwell writes that the function of myths "is to fulfill religious needs and is therefore both intellectual and emotional" (Edmunds 345). Otto Rank equates the protagonist in hero myths with the egos of children who rebel against the parents (84). The psychoanalytic school regards myths as "daydreams of the race, symbolizing a psychological and ethno-historical reality" (Patai 20) that expresses symbolically the processes of the unconscious. Freud wrote that dreams represent a function of the psyche which mitigates unwanted instinctual impulses. Dreams speak to people in symbols, and their images are found more visibly in myths. Myths then are "distorted vestiges of the wish-phantasies of whole nations—the age-long dreams of young humanity." Myths are the dreams of society, culture, and tradition (Doty 136). Dreams contain the symbols of individuals; myths the symbols of a group. Dreams for Freud represent the repressed psyche and therefore, myths too, are the repressed psyche of a group. Caldwell, like Freud, writes that societies "produce myths as dreams for the group," (7) and that "only these dreams that responded to the emotional needs of a large segment of the community could acquire the status of myth." Myths contain the memories of individuals and the collective stories of that group's history (*Ibid* 51).

Because of this interaction between the dream of individuals and the needs of the group, myths protect people from social fragmentation and bond them together emotionally (Caldwell 52). If myths are too remotely removed from their historical origins, then their stabilizing factor breaks down, as people no longer feel a rapport with the mythic stories and their symbols. The drawback with some psychoanalytic approaches is the tendency to view the images which arise from the unconscious as negative in character, being the products of repression, which attempt to evade the conflict between people's sexual urges and the moral and cultural constraints placed upon them (Jacobi 20-21). These at times may be valid views, but can fail to contribute to the life-affirming properties of the psyche as found in myths.

Mary Esther Harding wrote that the archetypes of the collective unconscious appear to people as images and typical events. These provide the themes of myths, and "they appear today in what Jung called 'big dreams,' using the term that some primitive peoples use to distinguish those dreams that have a collective import from the 'little dreams' that are of merely personal significance." These exist as energies in the "unknown psychic hinterland that determine the pattern of psychic experience much as the typical patterns that people call instincts determine the potentialities for biological experience" (*I & Not-I* 136). Harding wrote of Jung that he believed that all persons have a personal myth by which to live their lives, and that they need to discover what their own individual myth is, in order to "live it consciously and intelligently, cooperating with the trend of this life pattern, instead of being dragged along unwillingly" (*Ibid* 164). There are forces operating within the psyche, and depending upon people's degree of awareness, these forces will live the life of these people or they can live their own lives, by learning to cooperate, cultivate, and enhance their life's dramas. Rather than resisting the natural flow of life, these individuals will be assisting in their journey towards completion.

Although myths and dreams are often compared with one another, they are not exactly the same. Mythic images derive from the same "unconscious wells of fantasy, but they are not the spontaneous products of sleep. Their patterns are consciously controlled and function as a powerful picture language for the communication of traditional wisdom" (Campbell *Hero* 256). In these myths, "the continuance of the cosmic order is assured only by a controlled flow of power from the source. The gods are symbolic personifications of the laws governing this flow" (*Ibid* 261). Myths direct the "mind and heart to that ultimate mystery which fills and surrounds all existences. Even in the most comical and frivolous of its moments, mythology is directing the mind to this unmanifest which is just beyond the eye" (*Ibid* 267).

Furthermore, according to psychoanalytic theory, myths provide humanity with a medium by which to unravel repressed material, as well as revealing people's instinctual life, as they reflect the fantasies not only of individuals, but of whole nations. This repression begins during children's psycho-sexual development. It occurs as the result of children learning to act in a socially acceptable manner (Caldwell 19). Childhood sexuality includes all the desires and fantasies associated with organic pleasure not brought on by bodily needs, such as hunger. The desire and fascination with the objects which bring gratification continues after the physiological need has been met. Infants are able to displace the ego's desire onto objects other than the original one which brought gratification. These other objects become objects of fantasy (Edmunds 356). These fantasies revolve around themes of origin, existence, dependency, and separation (*Ibid* 357). These are certainly recurrent themes found in myths. Myths compensate for these newly perceived feelings of abandonment and the unknown. They reveal the journey of individuals through different psycho-sexual stages, and their attempt to regain what was lost at the advent of consciousness. The desire for union is really for a state, and not an object. However, objects supply the necessary symbols (*Ibid* 358) to which the desire may be transferred. Caldwell supports the notion that mystical union is equivalent to regaining the symbiotic state (26). I do not think that the mystical experience of union with the God-image of a Taoist sage or a Christian monk is by any means the same as the notion of people having an unconscious desire to "return to the womb." As Wilber points out, a return to a pre-natal state implies a condition that preceded self-consciousness (*Eye* 224). Self-consciousness brought with it separation anxiety. Mystics transcend self-consciousness and recognize a union with what is eternal. Thus, mystics are in a heightened state of awareness and do not regress to an earlier state of limited consciousness.

Freud stated that the Oedipus complex is at the heart of neurosis. It is the primary agent of infantile sexuality and affects adult sexuality as well (Eisner 3). These early psychosexual stages of life become repressed but not extinct. Freud believed that myths repeat the stages of infantile sexuality, and that repression is mitigated through fantasy. The myth of Narcissus represents the ego's need for total continuity. One's sense of self-worth is interpreted as being threatened. This is unconsciously associated with one's childhood feelings of inferiority (Brenner 240). The myth of Narcissus helps people to release themselves from a need for permanence. When individuals are less absorbed with feedback, they will be able to interact more autonomously. According to Freud, the Oedipus myth responds to the actions of a jealous son who loves his mother and kills his father. The Greek creation myths of Uranus-Gaia and Cronus-Rhea also display Oedipal themes of castration anxiety. This is due to the son's fear that his father will learn about his love for his mother and castrate him. The Oedipus tale reveals the importance of projecting the feelings onto a socially acceptable love object. Creation myths repeat the stages of the birth of the cosmos. These stages represent the psychological development of human beings. Psychoanalytic theory regards these myths as a reflection of the stages of infantile sexuality. All of these myths reveal anxiety over losing the self. The feelings associated with this loss of self remain unconscious, and as they are socially unacceptable are repressed.

Freud's major theory of this Oedipus myth is viewed differently from a Jungian perspective. Myths stand as metaphors to a deeper understanding of human beings. The falling in love with mother and then identification with father is not about real persons, but the energies in the psyche. Parents became the bearers of their children's images, those of nourishment, love, and care. Repression, especially religious, uses these parental images in a symbolic fashion, dressing them as archetypes (Frey-Rohn 154-155). The incest theme in myths, dreams, or fantasies is not about real parents, but about the movement in the psychic energies to break with the tribal mind. These energies separate people from the group consciousness and individuate in them uniquely. Jung wrote that "it was only the power of the 'incest prohibition' that created the self-conscious individual, who before had been mindlessly one with the tribe" (*CW* 5: 271). Additionally, Jung's use of symbols took something literal and personal and made it something figurative and impersonal. Symbolization releases the libido from incestuous chains and frees it for a spiritual journey (*Ibid* 226). Thus, contrary to Freud's notions, Oedipus myths are not about the desire to join physically with the human mother, but to return to a time of unconscious bliss and union with the archetypal Mother. This manner of regression is to an archetypal hinterland where images of gods, half animal, and semi-human beings dwell. These figures are far removed from the Freudian world of personal experiences and can be contacted only in the Jungian world of impersonal mythic images.

Campbell would not agree that these are myths' primary functions. He views myths as a function of transcendence moving human beings to self-actualization. Freud never thought that people could totally be free of Oedipal tendencies. Perhaps mystics transmute and project the Oedipal urges onto a symbol of universal proportion. Instead of being in love with a particular women, mystics might seek union with the image of a Mother Earth deity or female goddess figure. I do think that people must heal certain disorientations from the psyche before they will be ready to take the leap to psychic completion. Campbell said that "Freud's basic mistake was in trying to extend the situation of the infantile crisis and family romance to provide an interpretation of the totality of culture" ("Man & Myth" 39). Thus Freud is a good place by which to begin this healing process and Jung is the next step to healthy-mindedness.

Jung felt that moderns have lost contact with the voice Socrates relied on, his *daimon* or real self. This inner voice finds form in dreams and in myths (Leeming 317). People need to develop a mythical consciousness in order to travel more quickly their pathways to psychic integration. In order to be more complete, they must face the dark side of their natures, which is usually associated with the unpleasant aspects of human existence (*Ibid* 318). Thus, if they do not live with myths, sinking their roots deep into the ground, they will be deprived of nourishment from the collective unconscious.

Jung wrote that far into humanities' distant past, they had turned to rituals, dances, sacrifices, and their ancestral spirits, in order to "conjure up or reawaken those deeper layers of the psyche which the light of reason and the power of the will can never reach, and to bring them back to memory." Thus the use of mythological or archetypal ideas to aid in giving life to the unconscious (*CW* 14, 522). I do not think Jung is correct in making "mythological ideas" analogous to "archetypal ideas," in that the archetype is what generates the myths, which therefore are symbolic of the archetype. Mythic images follow archetypal pressure for release, and are thus their objective counterpart in which they must be interpreted in the particular milieu in which they impact. Wilber also makes a statement that "mythic images are not the archetypes" (*Eye* 242) in regards to Jung's synonymous usage of these terms.

The symbols of myths are not necessarily everlasting. Their representations can change from age to age, depending on the advances of consciousness that have occurred by new discoveries in science, changes in social attitudes, and personal growth experiences. When this happens, what was considered as real or true becomes superstition. People have seen this occur to the ancient civilizations of Egypt and Greece. No one still believes that there are gods on Mount Olympus. On the other hand, some mythic images do survive, but wear the clothes of the culture in which they now participate. The dragon slayer now battles with a corrupt corporation, or a journey across the sea is now a voyage through outer space (Jung *CW* 15, 97).

Lastly, as Jung concluded:

> Myths produce bridges between the helpless consciousness and the effective *idées forces* of the unconscious. But persons cannot, artificially and with an effort of will, believe the statements of myths if they have not previously been gripped by them. If they are honest, they will doubt the truth of those myths because their present-day consciousness has no means of understanding them. Historical and scientific criteria do not lend themselves to a recognition of mythological truth; it can be grasped only by the intuitions of faith or by psychology, and in the latter case although there may be insight it remains ineffective unless it is backed by experiences (*CW* 14, 528).

Chapter Three

The Symbol's Personhood: Heroes

Campbell wrote about the heroic journey and provided criteria to explain the patterns he discovered in myths that reflect this motif. Campbell explained that while the world's myths vary demonstrably in content, the metaphorical themes which run throughout them are quite similar. There is in essence but one spiritual heroic presence, but the world's cultures have given its heroic representatives many masks to wear. Each age has its heroic personages and they all undergo the same sort of spiritual journey or quest. They receive a call to adventure, answer it by undergoing arduous tasks and trials, overcome encounters with monsters, learn a better way of life, and return to tell or teach the world about this better way. Campbell defines "hero" as those persons who are able to push beyond their "personal and local historical limitations to the generally valid, normally human forms. The visions, ideas, and inspirations of such people come pristine from the primary springs of human life and thought" (*Hero* 19-20). These gladiators of the psyche must leave behind the attachments and comforts of their "old way" of life and enter an inner world while still participating in an outer world. This attitude is particularly prevalent in the character of Arjuna, whom will be dealt with in the analysis of the *Bhagavad Gita*.

Many people think that heroic figures are endowed with special abilities, far superior to most human beings. This is often the case in myths, as they are dominantly fictitious and written to reveal hidden truths supplying readers with the possibility of gaining insight into human nature. Thus the heroes and heroines of myths are representatives of the best of what human nature has to offer. The tales would hardly be interesting if the protagonists were ordinary. On the other hand, they must not be too superior or different, or the possibility of readers identifying with them would be limited. The one attribute that separates them from the rest of the world is the courage to face alone the forces of nature, society, and self. Campbell wrote:

> The agony of breaking through personal limitations is the agony of spiritual growth. Art, literature, myth and cult, philosophy, and ascetic disciplines are instruments to help individuals past their limiting horizons into spheres of ever-expanding realization. As they cross threshold after threshold, conquering dragon after dragon, the stature of the divinity that they summon to their highest wish increases, until it subsumes the cosmos. Finally, the mind breaks the bounding sphere of the cosmos to a realization transcending all experiences of form — all symbolizations, all divinities: a realization of the ineluctable void (*Hero* 190).

All heroic types must enter into the journey alone; no one can do it for them, although there can be helpers. Expanded awareness of the principalities operating in the world is a strong factor in moving beyond personal realms.

In *The Coming of the Cosmic Christ*, Matthew Fox discusses the self-sustaining attitude of mystics. I believe that the Campbellian idea of the heroic character applies equally well here. Fox writes:

> Mystics wrestle with the wars people carry on inside of themselves — the 'psychic battleground.' This provides a training ground for the social battles that need to be fought in the name of justice. The battles that mystics undergo teach a sense of personal understanding and compassion toward the 'enemy' that is missing when people have not confronted their own psychic battles. In other words, by confronting their projections and by healing psychic injustice, mystics clear the way for a more effective struggle for social justice. The scientific word for justice today is *homeostasis*, which is the quest for balance and equilibrium that is found in all organisms and even in the universe itself. Mysticism is about returning homeostasis to the human mind (62-63).

Thus those who are brave enough to plunge into the ocean of the unconscious will go through three stages of heroic development. These are "departure," "initiation" with its trials and victories, and "return" with a gift. This is a basic pattern objectified in myths, being the result of unconscious patterns in the human psyche. I recognize that this idea needs to be extended to show that this basic pattern is invariably repeated two or three times in the lives of some literary heroic characters. It may be repeated just as often or more in real life heroic types. The first journey of these three stages is a youthful one of apparent completeness, invariable followed by a second journey of three stages in adulthood, and often a third one in old age. Jesus had a call to adventure to follow the spirit of the law and not the letter of the law as laid down by Moses. He fought corruption and hypocrisy in the temple, and taught others about the kingdom of heaven. Later, Jesus had to answer a second call, to do the will of his Father and be a sacrifice for the sins of human beings.

As there are no authenticated writings of Jesus's teenage and young adult years, I must consider that his first call to adventure was when he began his ministry and his next when he faced the cross. In his case, he went through these stages twice in a short time. Most people, real or fictitious, move into their second journey later in life. For example, Oedipus answered a call to seek out the pollution in his land, even though it brought about his own expulsion. In *Oedipus at Colonus*, he answers an additional call as an old man who recognizes that love is the true foundation for peace. He is not afraid of dying and, in fact, is transformed into a benign spirit.

Departure is the call to adventure which beckons the latent heroes or heroines into an unplanned encounter with darkness, and at desperate moments with light bearing helpers. These adventurers learn to become their own teachers and saviours. This is where they make the break with family tradition and social mores. They stop conforming to the rules and patterns of thinking that have been conditioned by religious, parental, and cultural voices of authority when they conflict with their own inner voices of authority. To answer this call is to become free of the tangled web which society spins. They undergo initiations in pursuit of "real" knowledge, that is, knowledge of the self. These initiates follow the answering of the call with a departure from the safety and familiarity of earlier days. This begins their quest leading to a series of initiations.

The intrepids enter the darker places of the world: forest, swamps, caves, storm ridden seas; climb treacherous mountains, and trek overall hazardous paths. They travel through forests filled with beasts and traverse mountains and perilous bodies of water; but to survive actually means victory over the self: "The familiar life horizon has been outgrown; the old concepts, ideals, and emotional patterns no longer fit; the time for the passing of a threshold is at hand" (Campbell *Hero* 51). The initiates soon discover that there are benevolent forces everywhere operating to support them on their voyages to new worlds. Those who make the journey will find that they have special helpers in the most unexpected places. These helpers supply them with the proper information or tools to make their journeys successful (*Ibid* 36). Oftentimes what appears to be an ominous encounter or disastrous experience is but a test of these adventurers' convictions. At the moment they decided to set out on the quest, temptations seem to appear at every turn: a beautiful woman, jewels, and power; for Odysseus, the alluring cries of the Sirens who tempted him with knowledge (Eisner 205). Those who survive the journey are reborn, having died to an old way of life. Their journeys involve the slaying of outer influences that have restrained the soul (consciousness) from uniting with the eternal essence supplied by the spirit (unconscious).

The dauntless are initiated through a series of trials over which they must be victorious for the journey to be fulfilled. Those who dare the quest continuously sacrifice personal gain in service to the All. And this is the meaning of the word "sacrifice," to give up something of the lower path for something of the higher path. Campbell realized that the heroic types must sacrifice personal desire for universal compassion: They must die to their modern day image of the human and replace it with that of the eternal human—universal, integrated, unbounded—they have been made new. Campbell wrote that "those invested have been divested of their mere humanity and are representative of impersonal cosmic forces. They are twice-born: having become the mother or the father" (*Hero* 136-7).

It is not by accident that these adventurers seek out or end up at isolated spots, as these sites are shelters from the mundane and annoying activities of life (Eisner 205). It is quite necessary to retreat into isolation, to look deep within themselves in order to understand the answers that well up from the unconscious. They will encounter fierce creatures, evil omens, be tested as to physical dexterity, mental steadfastness, and spiritual and moral readiness. Keep in mind, these are mythological encounters, the scenes and creatures who fill these are symbolic of the struggles which occur within the psyche. These are the souls' battles with the archetypes and their demand for release into the objective world. Campbell so aptly put it this way:

> The references of the wild motifs are not really to the sun, the moon, the stars, to the wind and thunder, to the grave, to the hero, or even to the power of the group, but *through* these, back again to a state of the psyche. Mythology is psychology, misread as cosmology, history, and biography (*Wild Gander* 33).

The Greek warrior Odysseus had cunning, Hercules possessed strength, Oedipus was intelligent, and Jesus demonstrated keen spiritual insight and moral discipline. Most literary heroes and heroines are not real people and, therefore, the tales about them are one-sided, emphasizing one attribute at a time. Real life heroic personages are a combination of these attributes.

And the greater the power and richness of the symbols in the different tales, the more appealing they are to the human psyche, the more stimulating will be the calls to adventure.

It is written that "many are called, but few are chosen," and in fact most refuse their particular call. They are unprepared to make such an arduous journey and even less aware that they have been asked to make it. Many stay with the dead instead of letting them bury themselves. The attractiveness of the world is a powerful magnet, drawing the spiritually unenlightened to it. However, this call is also powerful and alluring. And those who answer it often feel themselves to be chosen. Sartre wrote in his autobiography *The Words*:

> I had taken precautions against accidental death; the Holy Ghost had commissioned me to do a long and exacting job, he had to leave me time enough to carry it out. [Death and I] had made a date; if I showed up too soon, it wouldn't be there yet (Eisner 204).

The Buddha's father, for example, surrounded him with all sorts of luxuries to keep him attached to the world, but to no avail. "When the student is ready, the teacher will appear," as happened to the Buddha. For he realized that "persons who are attached to the senses and things of this world, are those who live in ignorance and are being consumed by the snakes that represent their own passions" (Campbell *Wild Gander* 79). If people refuse the call, the positive forces turn against them and, instead of being a creative force, it can destroy, thus bringing about what Eliot called the "Waste Land."

"Their second solemn task is to return, transfigured, and teach the lessons they have learned of life renewed" (*Hero* 20). The adventurers have been dismissed from the enchanted world and enter back into normal life. This third stage of the heroic journey is called the return. Return is both a physical coming back and also a coming back with something to share with others. This is where the adventurers have overcome the trials of initiation and gained new insights about the world and about themselves. They seek to develop a rapport with their own internal psychic forces. Then the real gift that must be delivered to the world is awakening those who are asleep to their inner faculties. Succinctly put, those who return successfully are those who have undergone the process of becoming more fully conscious of the archetypal powers within them. "At the return threshold the transcendental power must remain behind; the heroic figures re-emerge from the kingdom of dread (return, resurrection). The boon that they bring restores the world (elixir)" (Campbell *Hero* 246).

Many after having become illuminated are quite doubtful as to whether or not anyone will listen to their message (Campbell *Hero* 193). Some enter into seclusion rather than attempt the difficult task of opening the minds of those who have known only how to seal them tight.

The Symbol's Personhood: Heroes

> That is the seeker's ultimate difficult task. How render back into light-world language the speech-defying pronouncements of the dark? How represent on a two-dimensional surface a three-dimensional meaning? How translate into terms of 'yes' and 'no' revelations that shatter into meaninglessness every attempt to define the pairs of opposites? How communicate to people who insist on the exclusive evidence of their senses the message of the all-generating void (*Ibid* 218)?

This is the idea behind Zen Buddhism, that the rational-conceptual mind will "miss the mark" of a spiritual target. It is even possible for the heroic figures to begin to doubt that what they experienced was true reality, for all evidence from the world will tend towards negation of the eternal. A Freudian interpretation of such a return might indeed leave the heroic travelers with the feeling that this was nothing more than the overcoming of a trauma and its associated pain. Certainly this perspective can service catharsis, but hardly permits a connection with the global significance of the event. Jung was aware that such experiences went further than personal confrontations and regarded myths as the value to be got from them. Jung regarded myths as well as the personality from a view of wholeness. He took into consideration the objective with the subjective, rational with irrational, impersonal with personal, and mundane with sublime. This regard encourages the release of transcendental energies, and for those with a successful return, they are channeled into the immanent. The Sioux Black Elk, the Ogala Keeper of the Sacred Pipe and a visionary to his people, said: "It is hard to follow one great vision in this world of darkness and of many changing shadows. Among these shadows humankind gets lost" (Campbell *Wild Gander* 112). Black Elk was but a boy of nine when he had his first vision which led to his becoming a great priest. The ways of his people were being destroyed by Western progress. As his people's sacred world was coming to an end, another vision told him that they must make a new one.

> Heroic ones must be masters of two worlds having the freedom to pass back and forth across the world division, from the perspective of the apparitions of time to that of the causal deep and back—not contaminating the principles of the one with those of the other, yet permitting

the mind to know the one by virtue of the other—are the talents of the masters. The Cosmic Dancer, declares Nietzsche, does not rest heavily in a single spot, but gaily, lightly, turns and leaps from one position to another (Campbell *Hero* 229).

The questing ones bring the human order into accord with the celestial. 'Thy will be done on earth, as it is in heaven.' The myths and rites constellate a mesocosm—a mediating, middle cosmos, through which the microcosm of individuals are brought into relation to the macrocosm of the universe. And this mesocosm is the entire context of the body social, which is thus a kind of living poem, hymn, or icon, of mud and reeds, and of the flesh and blood, and of dreams, fashioned into the art form of the hieratic city state. Life on earth is to mirror, as nearly perfectly as possible in human bodies, the almost hidden—yet now discovered—order of the pageant of the spheres. This pageant is what has shaped the mesocosm, the middle, sociological cosmos of the City; and the patterns of this mesocosm are what, then, have shaped the soul (Campbell *Wild Gander* 155).

Literature expresses the heroic journey using symbols personified in the world. The adventure takes place outside of the persons: in the forest, the cave, and so on. The monsters are creatures who inhabit the land, the gift is a magic ring or a potion. In reality, the heroic adventure takes place within the core of people's very beings. The symbols which arise and need translation and integration are from the unconscious. The real initiation is the decision to change the old way of perceiving and responding to the world. Such a decision requires that people replace old concepts with new ones and even transcend conceptual thinking altogether as do mystics. Part of this entails the mastery of feelings and the proper directing of them. The slain dragons are emotions from the psyche which had formerly not been properly guided. To return as heroes or heroines means to recognize an affinity with all life and to know that the forces and energies permeating the cosmos are part of and affect all expressions of life, whether mineral, vegetative, animal, or human.

Chapter Four

The Epic of Gilgamesh

I shall investigate four myths from various times and cultures in order to show the interplay of archetypes in them. The focus will be on the shadow, animus, anima, and self archetypes. In addition, The Campbellian stages detailing the protagonist's journey from departure, through initiation, to return will demonstrate the universal concept of the heroic figure. The Jungian ideas belonging to the archetypes and the Campbellian stages of the heroic journey will provide the methodology for analyzing the four myths.

These particular myths were chosen because of their cultural diversity, and also because of their archetypal resemblances. The protagonists in these myths are heroic in their responses to the critical moments of life. Their life-journeys reflect the three Campbellian stages of heroic development discussed in the previous chapter. Some of these heroes have followed their calling further than others; yet, they all answer the call to adventure, and in the process grow psychologically. *The Epic of Gilgamesh* comes down from the world of the ancient Near East and is the earliest account of an extant myth. The *Bhagavad Gita* is an early Hindu myth and reflects a developing religious system of the East. The Arthurian tale *Owein* reviews chivalresque customs of early medieval Europe, exemplifying the noble side of Western ideology. Lastly comes *Star Wars*, written in the twentieth century. *Star Wars* combines both Western and Eastern systems of thought into a unified whole. It reflects the technological age, and the values of human beings. There are numerous other myths that would fit this study just as well, but a discussion of them, while useful, is not necessary to understand the psychological structure of myths. The four myths with which I have chosen to work demonstrate from a variety of perspectives the common themes generated by the archetypes, which become manifest in the heroic journey.

Common to all these myths is the fact that they were written down and are now part of the present body of "mythopoeic" literature. Mythopoeic literature is important because it reflects archetypal energies unleashed from the unconscious. The closer the subjective framework of this material is to the unconscious, the more likely significant insights can be derived from the reading of or listening to these tales. Myths are, in part, deliberately constructed of symbols reflective of the archetypes.

J. B. Vickery made an important statement about the value of mythopoeic literature when he wrote:

> The mythopoeic i.e., mythmaking faculty is inherent in the thinking process, and its products satisfy basic human needs. Myths are the matrix out of which literature emerges, both historically and psychologically. As a result, literary plots, characters, themes, and images are basically elaborations and replacements of similar elements in myths and folktales. Theories of Jungian racial memory, historical diffusion, and the essential similarity of the human mind everywhere are among those resorted to in order to explain how myths reemerge in literature. To continue myth's ancient and basic endeavor to create a meaningful place for humankind in a world oblivious of their presence—this is the real function of literature (ix-x).

The Epic of Gilgamesh

The Epic of Gilgamesh has existed in written form for over four millennia, with the oral tradition dating earlier. These early Sumerian writings were discovered during the nineteenth century C.E. in Mesopotamia, in the form of scores of broken clay tablets covered with cuneiform (wedgeshaped) characters. Akkadian, Hittite, and Hurrian translations of the Sumerian epic have existed as far back as the second millennium B.C.E. It appears that the most important details of the story existed as ancient Sumerian poems (Sandars 8-13). The most complete version dated approximately 1600 B.C.E. is written in Akkadian and covers twelve tablets, which were found in the remains of the library of Ashurbanipal, the Assyrian king (668-

627 B.C.E) who assembled the greatest library of the pre-Hellenistic Near East in his capital, Nineveh (Tigay 11). Scholars believe that the Gilgamesh of the epic was a real person, the fifth king of the first post-diluvian monarchy of Uruk around 2700-2500 B.C.E. He was most likely a successful ruler who traveled to the cedar forests and returned with wood to be used in the construction of elaborate buildings. He was praised as a just judge and later became a "judge in the Underworld," to whom prayers were addressed (Sandars 21). Uruk was considered wealthy and a great temptation to invaders. Beautiful temples existed at which the king could converse with the gods, to whom he was their appointed regent on earth. These temples were presided over by priests, who were in charge of the riches kept there, and acted as teachers and scholars (*Ibid* 15). Following the death of Gilgamesh, the oral tradition related legendary and mythical tales regarding his life and lasted for five hundred years. The oral transmission of these tales was in Sumerian, and has been found in old Babylonian texts. Four of these Sumerian tales, "Gilgamesh and the Land of the Living;" "Gilgamesh, Enkidu, and the Netherworld;" "The Death of Gilgamesh;" and "Gilgamesh and the Bull of Heaven," along with additional narrative fragments, were compiled into the Akkadian epic (Jacobsen 242).

Gilgamesh's world was unstable, and thus had an aura of fear about it. The king was not viewed as being omnipotent and thus was mortal as was everyone else. The king received his scepter of authority from the gods, who acted with disregard for human life. The environment itself was unstable and famine was a threat. The name "Gilgamesh" even means sun-king (Jung *CW* 5: 171). The sun makes its journey from the dark into the light, repeating this cycle every day. Thus, the idea of a king who has successes and failures. People never knew which part of the cycle the sun-king was at. This may account for the pessimistic tone of the epic, which evolved from a tale about a particular hero to becoming a means for exploring the question of mortality and the way to cope with the feeling of dread associated with death. The epic has lasted for many centuries because it was written on durable clay, as well as reflecting the triumphs and tragedies common to human existence. The translation of *Gilgamesh* being used for this analysis was done by N. K. Sandars.

Gilgamesh is an heroic figure, two-thirds god and one-third human being, born of a father (Lugulbanda) who was half god, and therefore a mortal, and a mother who was a full goddess (Ninsun). Gilgamesh is endowed with talents and capabilities beyond any other person. As king of Uruk, he is a lustful playboy who wrestles with all the men and cohabits with their women. The citizens of Uruk pray to the gods to send someone who will intervene in this king's unruly behavior. The gods confer with each other and decide to send Enkidu, created out of a pinch of clay by Aruru, the goddess of creation. Enkidu is a savage who has a rapport with the animals of the forest with whom he runs wild, until being seduced by a harlot brought by a trapper from the city. After this seduction, of which Enkidu enjoyed the pleasures of a woman for seven days, he loses his innocence, and the animals now run away from him as they would from any human being. In addition, he is tired and incapable of keeping up with them. Jacobsen thought that this may be due, in part, because Enkidu

> is by then a bit tired; but almost certainly the author of the story saw more in it. The easy, natural sympathy that exists between children and animals had been Enkidu's as long as he was a child, sexually innocent. Once he has known a woman he has made his choice, from then on he belongs to the human race, and the animals fear him and cannot silently communicate with him as they could before. Slowly, Enkidu comprehends some of this. 'He grew up and his understanding broadened' (197).

Enkidu goes to Uruk when he hears that Gilgamesh is about to enjoy another man's bride at a wedding. He blocks Gilgamesh from entering into the house where the marriage ceremony will be performed, thus challenging Gilgamesh to what becomes a lengthy fight, from which Gilgamesh eventually emerges the victor. Reconciled, they become close friends and go off in pursuit of adventures that will bring them fame and restore to them their vitality. Gilgamesh has terrifying dreams which Enkidu erroneously interprets to mean the defeat of

Humbaba (Huwawa). Gilgamesh and Enkidu commit a series of thoughtless acts, which lead to the death of Enkidu. Gilgamesh, who is greatly overwhelmed by the loss of his friend, resolves not to suffer the same fate, and thus goes off, grieving, in search of immortality. Gilgamesh's travels take him over the perilous mountains, where he meets Siduri, a barmaid, who advises him that immortality was not meant for mortal man. Siduri tells Gilgamesh that it would be wiser for him to go home, raise a family and do the things that are common to all men. Gilgamesh ignores her words and continues, until he meets Urshanabi (Sursunabu), the ferryman of Utnapishtim (Ziusudra), who eventually lets him pass over the waters of death. Gilgamesh comes upon a reclining Utnapishtim and his wife (who remains nameless throughout the tale), the only survivors of the flood, who were bestowed with immortality. They inform Gilgamesh about a "plant of youth" which he succeeds in finding. Unfortunately, he sets the plant on the shore of a pond where he is swimming, and a snake comes along and eats it, thus shedding its skin and becoming young again. The story ends with Gilgamesh showing Urshanabi, the boatman of Utnapishtim, the great wall he has constructed around the city at Uruk. Gilgamesh, however, dies somewhat dissatisfied and resigned to his mortality.

The *Gilgamesh* epic describes the journey of Gilgamesh and his desire to be satisfied hedonistically, later to be successful, and then to be immortal. This necessarily requires him to undergo growth experiences. His development moves through three stages: first as a playboy and roughneck, second as one who seeks recognition by bringing back wood from the cedar forest, and third as one who acquires the "plant of youth," when it looks at least for a moment that he will gain his immortality. Bettelheim refers to Eliade, who thinks these experiences are symbolic journeys of *rites de passage*. All societies have their passages from childhood to adolescence, adolescence to adulthood, adulthood to old age, old age to death. Although passages are a physical dramatization, they are done to cultivate a psychological awareness. Some occur spontaneously, such as menstruation in females. Othertimes, the initiations are planned well in advance by the elders in a tribe, such as the passage of a mother-clinging boy to joining the hunt with the male members of his tribe. These initiation rites can be a metaphor for the "death of an old, inadequate self in order to be reborn on a higher plane of existence" (35). Joseph Campbell certainly thought that initiation rites were important to the lives of primitives in aiding them to break with maternal ties, and thus to become men. It is through these stories and the attending imagination that people experience certain perilous situations and confront arduous tasks in order to make the journey into the "Other World." Campbell included a story of primitive boys who crawled their way along a hard cold floor in total darkness to a cave, where, upon entering, the only sight they saw was of the shaman, painted on the cave wall. They moved along the umbilical cord of the cave floor into the maternal womb. And when they arrived, they were greeted by the father figure from whom a new and different nourishment was to come. One example of an initiation rite is represented by Enkidu's transformation from savage to man. This occurs when a harlot from the city seduces him, casting away his innocence as a savage (Sandars 30), because he now knows what it is like to be a human being.

I believe the psychoanalytic tradition would have seen Enkidu's sexual encounter as a social becoming. He is furthering his independence from the chthonic kingdom and entering into the paternal "civilized" world. The first sexual experience is always a turning point in people's lives. Jung's struggle with such psychoanalytic sexual theories facilitated his notions of "tension between opposites" and their eventual resolution (Frey-Rohn 140). As will become evident, the dynamics between the opposites is a recurring leitmotif in myths.

Gilgamesh's *rites de passage* cycle occurs in two parts which correspond to the Campbellian stages of departure, initiation and return. Gilgamesh's departure begins when Enkidu arrives at Uruk just before Gilgamesh is about to enter a wedding. Enkidu blocks Gilgamesh's passage into the home where the wedding is to be held and they begin to wrestle. Enkidu, though he is brought to one knee by Gilgamesh, is such a worthy opponent that Gilgamesh greatly respects him. Until the meeting of Enkidu, Gilgamesh had never encountered anyone to whom he could relate, as competitor, friend, or otherwise. Enkidu and Gilgamesh leave the city, away from culture, and together they wander into the untamed world. This is Gilgamesh's psychological break with tradition, custom, and human law, all of which he has spurned and conquered in one way or another. Thus begins their search for adventure. Gilgamesh now leaves his stagnant life in the city as playboy and roughneck, to explore another part of the world and himself. Now his human nature, less constrained by culture, finds itself among the more natural and primitive setting of the forecast. Gilgamesh's return to his source is the beginning of his discovering who he really is.

It is notable that Freud did not have such a positive outlook about such mythic moments. For he saw such episodes as the result of psychic trauma and the reacting to repressed memory traces from the past. Whereas Jung saw these episodes as uncovering meaning in their spontaneous response to the "developmental tendencies of the unconscious psyche" (Frey-Rohn 195). As Jung put it:

> Persons are only half understood when it is known how everything in them came into being. If that were all, they could just as well have been dead years ago. As living beings they are not understood, for life does not have only a yesterday, nor it is explained by reducing today to yesterday. Life has also a tomorrow, and today is understood only when persons can add to their knowledge of what was yesterday the beginnings of tomorrow (*CW* 7:46).

The initiation stage of this cycle is when Gilgamesh goes to the forest and encounters a variety of creatures by which he tests his strength. He and Enkidu battle the guardian of the forest Humbaba and, at Enkidu's coaxing, slay him. This senseless destruction throws the inhabitants of the forest into a panic. Soon afterwards, the goddess Ishtar, bedazzled by Gilgamesh's appearance, requests that he become her husband. Gilgamesh rudely rejects Ishtar and as she tells her father: "Gilgamesh heaped insults on me, he has told over all my abominable behavior, my foul and hideous acts." Ishtar is so enraged that Gilgamesh has pointed out to her that all the men she has had relationships with have come to a terrible fate. She is ready to smash open the gates of hell and bring the dead to eat with the living. Ishtar's father avoids this by giving her the "Bull of Heaven" to fight Gilgamesh. Gilgamesh and Enkidu welcome this new challenge and slay the Bull. Enkidu furthers the insult when he hurls the Bull's thigh at Ishtar. She then causes a seven year drought for those living in Uruk. This latest insult angers the gods greatly, thus they counsel and decide to put Enkidu to death, as he was the more ruthless of the two.

It is interesting that the departure and initiation stages are not the doings of a conscious or unconscious desire to fulfill a wish. Though Freud wrote that

> the motive forces of phantasies are unsatisfied wishes, and every phantasy is the fulfillment of a wish, a correction of unsatisfying reality (*SE* 9: 146-47).

The analytical tradition views this phenomena as a result of deep psychic energies at work and whether wishes come true or not, they are not the motive forces propelling a mythic journey. Gilgamesh's quest was not the result of a wish-fulfillment to enter the forest and conquer. He was responding to unconscious creative tendencies of which he was not yet mindful.

The return stage of this first heroic cycle is the sense of self-importance Gilgamesh experiences as a conqueror of monsters and nature. Unfortunately for him, however, this success suffers a reversal and results in his immediate suffering. True, he has proven his physical prowess, but he has failed miserably at being a person with any common sense or empathy for others. His heroism is strictly physical at this point and will need to be spiritualized if his life is to be meaningful.

The cycle repeats itself at a higher level of development during Gilgamesh's second departure or call to adventure. This second departure and Gilgamesh's unconventional heroism develop after the death of Enkidu, when for the first time Gilgamesh experiences defeat. Gilgamesh lives at a time when heroic, courageous acts of strength appear to be the norm, at least by certain individuals. To face death is not an unusual scenario; however, up until the time of Enkidu's death, Gilgamesh thought about it in the abstract. When Enkidu died, reality sank in and brought with it his existential despair (Jacobsen 202-203). A Freudian might view such an event as a trauma resulting from Gilgamesh's somewhat boyish ego. He had never been emotionally prepared for such a tragic moment. This is why Gilgamesh departs dazed and confused. He is not repressing what has happened, as he is quite aware that he is alone now. But does not have the psychological maturity to handle such a shock to his system.

The time when the "singing girls crowded round to admire Gilgamesh" after he and Enkidu had slain the Bull, satisfied his desire for fame (Sandars 35). Enkidu's death, however, caused Gilgamesh to question personal success as being inadequate, and thus he moves to the next part of his quest. This is where a Jungian might view Gilgamesh's mourning over his friend as transforming him from one who seeks after fame, to one who seeks after that which will let him defeat death: wisdom. He now realizes that like Enkidu, he is mortal and so becomes obsessed with finding a way to defeat death and become immortal like Utnapishtim.

The primary difference I see between a Freudian and a Jungian explication of Gilgamesh's reaction to Enkidu's death is that a Freudian might attribute Gilgamesh's wandering about as the result solely of an external event, leading to a trauma. Whereas a Jungian might see the external event as secondary to the perpetuating archetypal life energy. The trauma Gilgamesh experiences is one of many possible responses to this energy. The outer event acts only as a catalyst for what has been brewing a long time.

Now begins Gilgamesh's second initiation cycle. He roams the earth in seeming disarray, wearing the skins of wild animals, as he himself has fallen to his lowest level of despair. His humanness lies buried within his grief and confusion; losing contact with culture, losing touch with reason, he lives off of the land and acts instinctively as do the animals. He comes into contact with the barmaid Siduri who tells Gilgamesh to eat, drink, and be merry, for human beings are meant to die, so enjoy life while possible. Gilgamesh is unable to accept this attitude, so he continues his search for where Utnapishtim lives. He is carried across the river of death by

Utnapishtim's ferryman Urshanabi, bringing him beyond the boundaries of the known world. It is here that he meets Utnapishtim and his wife, the only survivors of the flood. Utnapishtim tells Gilgamesh that if he can overcome sleep, the cousin of death, for seven days, he will find the life for which he is searching. However, Gilgamesh fails this test. He grows somewhat despondent, and Utnapishtim's wife feeling sympathy for him, sees to it that he is informed about the whereabouts of the "plant of youth."

This is the ending initiation with its final trial and the movement to the second return cycle. Gilgamesh is directed to the "plant of youth," finds it, and decides to wait to consume it until he can share it with others. This is an important passage because he is extending himself. He is no longer the selfish child-like ruler, whose "arrogance has no bounds [and] lust leaves no virgin to her lover." He moves from a potential long and youthful life back to man when the snake devours the plant and sheds its skin (Sandars 62).

The "plant of youth," also called "the plant which makes one to be young again," is, I believe, a plant of immortality. It is eaten once and one lives forever, that is, is made young again, forever young. Thus one becomes immortal, like the gods. In fact, one would be a god and have usurped the powers of nature. Most heroic adventurers do not live forever; instead, they resign themselves to their mortality, as did Hector and Achilleus, but complete tasks which make them famous, and die. Jesus and Hercules are exceptions, but then again, their tasks on earth were exceptional; one would even say, godlike, and thus they have been treated as gods.

Jacobsen reflects keenly that

> throughout the epic Gilgamesh appears as young, a mere boy, and he holds on to that status, refusing to exchange it for adulthood as represented by marriage and parenthood. Like Barrie's Peter Pan he will not grow up. His first meeting with Enkidu is a rejection of marriage for a boyhood friendship, and in the episode of the bull of heaven he refuses—almost unnecessarily violently—Ishtar's proposal of marriage. She spells disaster and death to him. So when Enkidu dies, he does not move forward seeking a new companionship in marriage, but backward in an imaginary flight toward the security of childhood. At the gate of

the scorpion man he leaves reality; he passes literally 'out of this world.' In the encounter with the alewife he firmly rejects marriage and children as an acceptable goal, and eventually, safely navigating the water of death, he reaches the ancestors, the father and mother figures of Utnapishtim and his wife, where, as in childhood, age and death do not exist. True to his images, Utnapishtim sternly attempts to make Gilgamesh grow up to responsibility; he proposes an object lesson, the contest with sleep, and is ready to let Gilgamesh face the consequences. The wife of Utnapishtim, as mother, is more indulgent, willing for Gilgamesh to remain a child, and she eventually makes it possible for him to reach his goal with the plant 'As Oldster Man Becomes Child.' Gilgamesh is fleeing death by fleeing old age, even maturity; he is reaching back to security and childhood. The loss of the plant stands thus for the loss of the illusion that one can go back to being a child. It brings home the necessity for growing up, for facing and accepting reality. And in the loss Gilgamesh for the first time can take himself less seriously, even smile ruefully at himself; he has at last become mature (218-29).

Gilgamesh's personality continuously reflects these growth experiences. His character is better than most: "When the gods created Gilgamesh they gave him a perfect body, beauty, courage. Two-thirds they made him god." And this is how Gilgamesh ends his journey, two-thirds complete. He does not reach the pinnacle of a Jesus or Buddha. He lacks the spiritual insight and attitude to complete his quest for life everlasting. The best heroic personages move beyond "what can life do for me" to "what can I do for life."

As Gilgamesh is maturing, unfolding, and integrating his personality, he feels distraught. He does not recognize why he feels this way. His lack of discernment and wisdom is his flaw. This may, in part, be due to the Mesopotamian mind-set and to "a haunting fear that the unaccountable and turbulent powers may at any time bring disaster to human society" (Gresseth 3). His inability to be introspective explains his self-aggrandizement. Even Gilgamesh's own people call upon the gods to intervene for his unbecoming activity as the king (Sandars 62). When Gilgamesh suffers, and seeks fulfillment anew, his true heroism is recognized. He is a hero because he faces overwhelming odds and tries until the last to be immortal. His partial success comes from building the wall at Uruk. This monument may not satisfy his longing for physical immortality, but it does satisfy his historical immortality.

There are faint glimmerings in this myth of success themes. To the degree Gilgamesh succeeds, there is hope, and to the degree he fails, there is despair. His failure in not the result of interfering gods, uncaring humans, or lack of personal talents, but an inability to reason effectively and empathize with the various creatures he encounters. The unconscious can be like a tumultuous lava bed ready to release its pent-up energy. To the degree Gilgamesh's consciousness is unable to integrate the pressure from the unconscious, his thinking and behavior is indecisive. He lacks motility to achieve a balance between these two aspects of his psyche.

There is an evolving scheme in the Gilgamesh story focusing on characters and events surrounding the release of archetypes from the unconscious and integrating them into consciousness through the experiences of the various characters. He does not integrate his archetypes sufficiently, which brings me to an analysis of Gilgamesh's psyche. His shadow predominantly rules his life up to the time of Enkidu's death. His shadow is found in the characters he encounters in the world. It is not that they are evil, but that Gilgamesh projects his own shadow onto them. This is why he ruthlessly conquers those who remind him of civilized behavior. He is reacting against these others because of the immature development of his consciousness. He mistakenly perceives them as hostile forces to be confronted and destroyed. Humbaba represents an archetype of protection, and acts as a censor for those who trespass on the forest, which is symbolic of the unconscious. Gilgamesh denies this part of himself when he slays Humbaba, because he is not yet mature enough to recognize this archetype. The deaths of Humbaba, the Bull of Heaven, and the increased rage of Ishtar, are due to ignoring the dark side of the shadow. This would explain Gilgamesh's lust for women, his uncaring attitude toward his subjects, and his destructive-aggressive nature as when he slays Humbaba. When Gilgamesh slays Humbaba (a symbol of the father), he may actually be stifling the voice of authority within himself. It takes Gilgamesh a long time before he realizes that he must make friends with his shadow, that is, the destructive side of himself. The projections he throws onto so-called monsters are really parts of himself with which he needs to be reconciled. The beasts Gilgamesh encounters in the forest are personifications of the untamed forces within himself, in his psyche. When he kills Humbaba, he is becoming the master of nature, its subduer, but not its friend; and thus, not a friend to his own natural inclinations and forces. Gilgamesh and Enkidu are both children who must grow up and be socialized. Gilgamesh acts out male imperatives for aggression in order to avoid the fact that he will die (Beye 41). Gilgamesh has failed to fit into the world of culture and the world of nature. It is not until the end of the tale, where he accepts his mortality and gazes upon the wall he has built at Uruk, that he reconciles these opposing forces within himself and thus has a rapport with the world. As long as he is the knight who slays dragons, he cannot mature psychologically, because he ignores the parts of himself that frighten him. Once he recognizes that the shadow can be his friend, he can enjoy the world and work with it in cooperation, not competition.

Gilgamesh rebukes the authority of Ishtar, exemplary of love on the positive pole and uncontrollable passion on the negative pole. Ishtar is the personification of his anima archetype. If Gilgamesh accepts Ishtar when she is passionate, he would be feeding his hunger for sensual gratification. To reject her so abruptly is to reject the passion within himself and thus to try to deny now this unruly side of himself. Gilgamesh also refuses to marry Ishtar because he is afraid to be her husband and thus a ruler of the Netherworld. The Netherworld is full of chaos, symbolic of the chaotic elements of the unconscious. Gilgamesh is not yet mature enough to govern them. Thus if he is overpowered by the anima (accepts Ishtar too brashly), it can destroy him. If he refuses her completely, his opportunity for regeneration may pass-by him. Ishtar is a precarious figure, representing both fertility and life, but also the "cause of death and the receiver of the dead" (Abusch 159). Even the Bull which usually represents life is sent to destroy. Ishtar is a very contradictory figure, and like the anima, there are two sides to her. Thus marriage implies leaving behind one mode of being and entering into another. Funerals are this way too. Gilgamesh treats Enkidu as a bride at his funeral when it is read: "He covered the face of this friend as if he were a bride" (Abusch 157-8). Thus for Gilgamesh to join Ishtar, the goddess of the Netherworld, is to join death—the thing he fears most (Abusch 161). It is the manner in which Gilgamesh rejects Ishtar which shows his lack of discernment in his judgments. However, his rejection also acknowledges his strong sense of masculinity and psychological stability of his ego. He does not feel a need to link himself to a woman in order to be fulfilled (Neumann *Origins* 63). Gilgamesh wants to be regenerated without the aid of a female (*Ibid* 182). The only women he has healthy encounters with are his own mother and Utnapishtim's wife, a mother figure, who cares for him. She helps make the location of the "plant" known to him, thus enabling him to return to the youthful existence of a "child." In any case, the persona or mask he exposes to the world is a false one, and leads to his alienation from the world. To marry Ishtar when she is expressing her loving side is to unite the diverse forces of his personality. But this side of her is never witnessed, and thus the possibility of this spiritual marriage taking place does not occur. It is only by making friends with himself that he is able to make friends with the world and its innate forces. Gilgamesh has not yet learned to be in touch with the part of himself which expresses love; he therefore identifies with the passionate side of Ishtar and reacts accordingly. She mirrors the unruly nature of Gilgamesh to himself, and, as he is yet unable to accept responsibility for his internal development, he angrily rejects her. Only after Enkidu's death does a movement toward personality integration, which expresses as a quest for immortality, come into full force.

Enkidu and Gilgamesh each personify the animus. They are strong, brash, fearless, and like to get into trouble. Enkidu, the untamed man who recklessly encourages destruction wherever he goes, stimulates Gilgamesh in his destructiveness. The creation of Enkidu by Aruru is a warning to Gilgamesh that he needs to mature and cease his recklessness, as he is essentially challenging the gods, which no human being may do and survive. However, Gilgamesh does not see Enkidu as the untamed part of himself, personified, but only as a special friend to join forces with and run wild. Humbaba warns Gilgamesh that Enkidu speaks evil words, but Gilgamesh does not heed him and listens instead to Enkidu, causing confusion in the forest. Enkidu is thus also a reinforcement of Gilgamesh's shadow. They have a strong animus bond as is evident from their urgency to cling to each other after wrestling. This foreshadows the drama of their later separation (Beye 42). They are really brothers, and Gilgamesh even refers to Enkidu as his brother. This is why they have a strong psychological rapport; and when the two of them join forces, lacking well-balanced personalities, they become unconquerable and cruel. As Enkidu is a physically grounded person, he also reinforces Gilgamesh's animus and his sense of masculine adventure.

Gilgamesh's self archetype demands him to be all that he is able to be, and perhaps more than he is able to be. Gilgamesh identifies himself with the gods who are the beings closest to being complete. They live forever and have supernatural powers though, from their defeats at the hands of Gilgamesh and Enkidu, they are not omnipotent. It is here that Gilgamesh and Enkidu suffer from ego-inflation. Their egos mistakenly believe that they are now god-like. When in fact the journey is far from being over. The self is suggesting only potentials to be unfolded throughout the long process of individuation. Their error in understanding causes them much grief.

Regardless, the self archetype projects Gilgamesh's objective of immortality, which is foreshadowed throughout the myth. An example of this is when Gilgamesh discusses encountering Humbaba, and says: "Then if I fall I leave behind me a name that endures." He continues: "All the world shall know of it. I am committed to this enterprise: to climb the mountain, to cut down the cedar, and leave behind me an enduring name." Thus, Gilgamesh must seek a way to live conducive to his personal energy and simultaneously to act responsibly. This includes fitting into society and learning about himself and accepting his mortality (Abusch 144).

The mourning over Enkidu is Gilgamesh's bereavement over the gradual loss of his old self. The mourning lasts a long time because Gilgamesh is unable to let go of his old inadequate self. When he later accepts the death of Enkidu, he is accepting life for himself. To the extent Gilgamesh remains in limbo between his old and new self, he lacks full participation in and understanding of life. The barmaid Siduri is perhaps the best example of a personality who is well balanced. She is quite comfortable where she is and with what she does. At the same time, she is not apathetic like Utnapishtim, who "lays at ease." She gives sound, prudent advise to Gilgamesh, motivated neither by unruly desires nor grandiose expectations. She is able to reason upon the various possibilities for her existence and arrive at a sound conclusion. This is something Gilgamesh has yet to learn to do. Utnapishtim, although like Gilgamesh in appearance, appears passive, indicating that there is nothing anyone can do to have the favor of the gods. This attitude reveals to Gilgamesh the futility of happiness being found in immortality. The great message in the story in thus not so much to give up the quest, but to integrate the personality in such a way that the quest is recognized as being fulfilled here and now, not something which occurs in another time or place.

The death of Enkidu was the shock required to arouse Gilgamesh from his psychological slumber of indifference. This was the death of his own fun-loving self. He finally learns that this approach to life is ephemeral and can have most disastrous consequences. He is like the alcoholic who has awaken once too often, not knowing where, and decides it is time to get control of his life. For Gilgamesh, controlling his life means to control nature. Prior to Enkidu's death, Gilgamesh had been self-centered and focused on the fruits of the world, living as a hedonist. Oftentimes, people will refuse to listen to the beckoning inner voice, because the materiality and passion of the world shouts to them from every corner. People meditate and pray in order to silence the distractions of the world, closing off the receptivity of their sense, so as not to be led astray from a path of compassion. Another way people enter into themselves is the way of Gilgamesh, through tragedy. Gilgamesh's mourning over Enkidu caused him to withdraw from the world and enter into his own silence. In confronting his personal loss and its associated pain, he began to question the mystery of life and seek out a way to make life meaningful. In seeking not to suffer the same fate as his friend, Gilgamesh eventually made his life meaningful.

This tale is a good example of how the protagonist, engrossed in the world, by satisfying his lust for women, power, fame through killing monsters, takes a long time to realize that changes in the world always follow changes of the heart. Even when Gilgamesh meets Utnapishtim and is given the plant of youth by which he is able to become young again, he loses it to a snake. The supposed boon he is to bring back to his people in the form of this magic elixir is lost. It is not until this last calamity that he realizes the boon to be shared is not a thing, a magic potion, but himself, his wisdom, his newly matured nature. All great teachers, Jesus, Buddha, Socrates gave themselves, not things, to the world. Granted, the wall at Uruk he constructed is a thing, but it is created by a Gilgamesh who is able to gaze upon it from a new perspective. He may not be as great and psychically integrated as a Jesus, Buddha, or Socrates, but he was handed the riddle of life and solved a good portion of it.

Chapter Five

Bhagavad Gita

The *Bhagavad Gita*, also known as "the Song of God," is an eighteen chapter dialogue between the god Krishna, who is the eighth incarnation of the god Vishnu, and the Pandu Prince Arjuna. The *Gita* is a seven hundred verse sacred text and part of the one hundred thousand verse *Mahabharata*, meaning "Great India." There is no exact dating of the *Gita*, though it is believed to have been written around 300 B.C.E. Vyasa is considered by some to be the author of the *Mahabharata*, though nothing is known of him. The *Gita* may be referred to as an extension of the *Vedas*, meaning a scripture which discusses the truth. The *Vedas* from the word *"vid"* mean knowledge. They are also called *shruti*, meaning "that which is heard." Truth heard in the deepest of meditations. Thus that the content of these Vedic truths (*shrutis*) are known as the *Sanatana Dharma* or truth that is eternal, not relevant to one time or place, but to all times and places. *Sanatana Dharma* is a more appropriate way to refer to this Indian philosophy, though many know it as Hinduism. The reference to Hinduism derives from associating its origin with the Indus Valley (Satchidananda xiii).

The background to the *Gita* begins with a girl called Satyavati copulating with a terrible smelling ascetic. She was unable to bear him any longer, thus at the moment of conception she shut her eyes, and was told that because of this her son would be very strong, but born blind. His name is Dhritarashtra, and he is the eldest son in a royal family. Again Satyavati was put through the same ordeal, and in the act of intercourse went pale. Thus her son was born pale and was called Pandu, meaning white. As Dhritarashtra is blind, his younger brother Pandu assumes the throne. Pandu had five sons, of whom Arjuna is the second. Dhritarashtra had one hundred sons, of whom Duryodhana is the eldest. The battle is between Pandu's sons, the Pandavas, and Duryodhana's sons, their cousins, called the Kauravas. Pandu died at an early age, thus his brother Dhritarashtra took power, treating his own children leniently and his nephews severely. As the Pandavas exhibited many admirable qualities, their cousin Duryodhana became envious. Due to treachery on the part of Duryodhana, the Pandavas were banned from their kingdom.

The *Gita* begins with Arjuna, one of the five Pandu brothers, about to engage in a great battle at Kurukshetra, over the territory of Hastinapura, ruled by the Pandu princes' cousin Duryodhana, acting for his blind father Dhritarashtra. Now, Arjuna and his brothers return to reclaim their land and decide to fight their kinfolk known as the Kauravas. Krishna is sought independently by Duryodhana and Arjuna. He offers either a great army or his services as charioteer driver to the opposing cousins. Duryodhana decides the army is better to have, and Arjuna decides that he would rather have Krishna accompanying him. Arjuna asks the god Krishna to drive him to a place where he can watch the battle, as he is stunned at the thought of entering into it against his friends and cousins. Arjuna does not understand how all the riches of the world could be worth their death. The story is about this confusion in the mind of Arjuna and the philosophical discourse that takes place between him and Krishna, a god who views life from an absolute perspective. Arjuna eventually consents to play his role in this drama, which makes his party victorious.

I shall now briefly summarize each chapter. The story opens with Arjuna anguishing over whether to enter the imminent battle between his kinfolk. It is then that Krishna, acting as his charioteer, begins his discourse with Arjuna.

Both Freud and Jung recognized that such psychic conflict as Arjuna's resulted from polar tension. This myth is particularly strong in its use of opposites. Freudians might view Arjuna's dilemma as resulting from repressed unconscious material causing him trauma. However, Arjuna seems quite aware of a problem, though he has yet to recognize the solution to it. Jungians most probably would regard Arjuna's situation as a stepping stone to further individuation. His outer world actions are responsive to unconscious psychic proddings. Freudians view these proddings as contributing to neurosis. That is, the ego (Arjuna) is too weak to confront the repressed unconscious material (kinfolk) and thus becomes inactive (Arjuna's indecisiveness). There is no particular growth in such an interpretation, only a condition of temporary homeostasis for the ego. Contrariwise, Jungians believe neuroses to be part of the normal human experience and when successfully managed lead to creative development. There is nothing negative here except to an ego failing to acknowledge the problem and work through it. In fact, it is the ego which views polar tension as negative because it conflicts with its ordinary perspective on how things are and thus disturbs its comfort zone (the habits and patterns it is addicted to). Neurosis means that the unconscious self (Krishna) has been busy knocking on the door of the conscious ego (Arjuna). Only when the ego cowers from opening the door does the psyche's energy increase its demand to be let in. Once the door is opened and this unconscious stranger welcomed, a great friendship can develop. Arjuna's task will be to make friends with the enemy.

Chapter two introduces the concept of *dharma*. Krishna tells Arjuna that there is no reason to feel sorrowful, as the wise do not grieve for the dead nor express pity for the living. Regardless of what happens to the body, the soul is immortal and thus impossible to slay. Krishna reminds Arjuna that as a member of the *kshatriya* or warrior caste, he must fight. It is Arjuna's duty to act as a warrior, and in so doing keep the Kauravas from doing further injustice. The idea of *karma* yoga is introduced and continued in chapter three. *Karma* yoga, like most forms of yoga, is experiential. It insists that action is a necessary condition of living, and is best done when the actors are detached from the results.

In chapter four Krishna tells of the many times He comes to earth as an avatar helping in times of crisis. In His various guises, He repeats ancient wisdom in the tongue of that present age. *Karma* yoga is part of this wisdom which says that there can be action in inaction, and inaction in action. For example, a man may plant corn seeds at an improper time of the year for them to take root and they die. Thus there was inaction in his action. A woman may remain calm and patient towards an angry employer, who is venting his frustration on her. Her inaction could result in her keeping her job, and thus there was action in her behavior. Jung saw the psyche as having a type of karmic reflex. And referred to the archetypes as "regularly occurring events in the soul's cycle of experience" (*CW* 7: 95). He further wrote in a footnote that "the archetypes may be regarded as the effect of experiences that have already taken place, but equally they appear as the factors which cause such experiences" (*Ibid*). For Jung, karma implied destiny. And it is Arjuna's destiny that will either propel him to fight or flee.

Chapter five speaks of the renunciation of desires. The Real Self is unaffected by the bodily appetites or mental yearnings. This leads nicely to chapter six and the practice of meditation. Initiates are to focus on the Real Self or Atman, and the union with Brahman. These disciples should follow the middle path, neither being excessive nor slothful in action.

Krishna's cosmic nature is revealed in chapter seven through the concepts of *maya* (illusion), the *gunas* (qualities), and *prakriti* (matter). Those who identify with Krishna will learn that their own nature is like His. Jung understood this when he wrote "the historical, universal person within joins hands with the newborn, individual person" (*CW* 8:380). It is the concept of *maya* that causes people to perceive objects and themselves as separate entities. Actually there is only one reality, the Absolute, Atman-Brahman. *Maya* is a type of force or power that gives the appearance that there are the Many, when there is really only the One. The astronomer Carl Sagan says that human beings are made out of "space stuff," and that the trees are cousins, and the stars are grandparents. Physicists recognize that all life is made from the same subatomic particles. They group together to form different patterns, thus giving the impression that life's forms are quite different, when in essence they originate from the same basic building blocks. As Frey-Rohn declares:

> Whenever individuals experienced the deeper significance of collective images and the connection with the existing store of experiences had been established, it was equivalent to a reunion with the source of life. Individuals felt themselves as one with the greater in their psyches. What they experienced was the mystery of again putting together what had been separated (124).

Krishna is the bridge to Arjuna experiencing this mystery and regaining the lands of not only his outer kingdom but the inner as well.

In chapter eight Arjuna learns that Brahman is without a predecessor. Brahman appears as Atman in an individual, when in essence the two are the same. They are really Atman-Brahman (Worthington 63). Arjuna is told to meditate on the sacred syllable *AUM (OM)*. It is composed of three sounds representing *Trimurti*. *Trimurti* is the idea that God manifests in three divine forces. These are Brahman the creative force, Shiva the destructive force, and Vishnu the preserving force. These three forces work together to perpetuate the cycle of birth, death, and rebirth. *AUM* is often chanted as part of a mantra. A mantra is a sacred word or phrase that is spoken during meditation to center the thoughts on the Real Self or Ultimate Reality, freeing the initiates from *maya*. *AUM* represents waking, dreaming, and dreamless sleep with the silence being the period of creative regenerativity. Out of the silence comes the rebirth of the universe. The world of "sound" is the universe of the physically manifesting. Silence is antecedent to sound. Campbell wrote about sound as being a potential of the "primal Silence." And that space-time is a potential contained within the Great Void (*Myths To Live By* 114). When Brahman is breathing in, the universe is still and silent, and when this Creating Force is breathing out, the world is busy and noisy. Meditating can facilitate a return to the silence and stillness before creation.

Chapter nine reveals that everything exists within Brahman. During the nights of Brahman all creation sleeps, and during the days it awakes again in an endless cycle (Worthington 64).

These cycles are of quite long duration, usually a thousand *Yugas* (an age of the world) or one *Brahm* (four billion years).

Chapter ten sings of praise to Atman-Brahman, and Their incarnating Krishna, who are antecedent to the manifesting universe. And in chapter eleven Arjuna beholds the entire universe in all its magnificence through the radiating Krishna.

The twelfth chapter discusses the devotional yoga known as *bhakti*. Bhakti yoga emphasizes love and worship of Brahman or one of Its incarnations, rather than the doing of ablutions, sacrifices, offerings, or other religious rituals.

In chapter thirteen Arjuna learns that he must enter his own center, transcending *prakriti* and join with Brahman. *Prakriti* is the concept that the physical world is composed of twenty-four principles, with these divided into the three *gunas*. The continuously changing *prakriti* must be united with the unchanging spiritual essence known as *purusha*. The union of the two brings about self-consciousness in human beings. Body/matter (*prakriti*) must join with soul/spirit (*purusha*).

The three *gunas* or qualities are discussed in chapter fourteen. They are *sattva* or wisdom; *rajas* or passion; and *tamas* or ignorance. These give structure to the physical world, binding it together. The *gunas* are responsible for the emotional temperament and actions of human beings. Human behavior will be determined by which of three *gunas* or combination of these are interacting.

Chapter fifteen mentions the *asvattha* or sacred fig tree, with its roots in heaven and its branches on earth. Its leaves represent the *Vedic* knowledge (sacred literature). Those with understanding will recognize that the world is forever changing. It is an impermanent dwelling place of the soul. The universe is like a river forever flowing, in flux. Heraclitus stated that no one can step in the same river twice. The river appears to be the same, but in reality is different from moment to moment. Those who wish to be liberated from their *karmic* cycle must detach themselves from such illusion, and by so doing experience *moksha* or release. *Moksha* is freedom and the end of reincarnating, by the recognition of Atman and its union with Brahman.

Chapter sixteen describes the nature of morality and immorality. It suggests how the initiates can avoid wrong action and what they must do to perform right action.

The *gunas* are again mentioned in chapter seventeen in regards to how they affect people's worship. Those of *sattva* will worship Brahman; those of *rajas* material possessions; and those of *tamas* the ghosts of their ancestors (Worthington 67). The mantra of *OM TAT SAT* is chosen when worshipping Brahman. *Om* has been discussed in detail already. It also means the "living force that represents the supreme Lord." *Tat* is that which is self-existent, and *Sat* is Absolute Reality. Together they are a reminder of that which is self-sustaining (Rama 424).

The final chapter eighteen is about the yoga of renunciation and the giving up of the attachment to the fruits of action.

Please note that quotes cited in this chapter from the *Gita* have been translated by Yogi Ramacharaka. While doing this investigation, it is helpful to realize that those remaining true to their *dharma*, whether winners or losers in war, are victors, spiritually. The battlefield is the setting for the real story, which is the battle within Arjuna, the conflict of his soul with his social indoctrinations. Hermes wrote: "The soul must begin by warring against itself, and stirring up within itself a mighty feud and the one part of the soul must win victory over the other." One part attempts to climb upwards while the other part voraciously seeks to drag it down (Bryce 47). The *Gita* teaches through symbols the stages that individuals must undergo in the "heroic journey of self-discovery" (Rama 11). This myth is about *sadhana* or the spiritual practice which leads the aspirants to attain internal peace and harmony with the outer world, while learning the yogic way of performing acts efficiently and selflessly (Rama 2).

In more psychological language the battlefield is where the armies of the collective unconscious is released in this ultimate challenge of the mobilizing group spirit to draw the personal spirit of Arjuna into surrendering to these unconscious forces. It requires the warrior's strength to permit union with the unconscious. The final surrendering of the ego, the giving up of ephemeral attachments, is what brings victory to the soul.

The personal ego must join with the archetypal impersonal self, and in doing achieve the guided balance necessary for sagehood. Jung, by recognizing myths to be products of the impersonal energies, lifted what otherwise might have been personal tragedy to a creative sphere. Personal conflicts must be healed, and can be made less of a struggle by drawing on ancestral energies. Those who rely solely on personalistic interpretations of their journeys will suffer poorly from so narrow a view.

Krishna discusses the wisdom of the *Vedic* and *Upanishadic* literature (ancient Hindu sacred writings) through the *Gita*. He does not invent a new philosophy, but paraphrases and extends an ancient one in his dialogue with Arjuna, the symbol of humanity (everyman) (Rama 4). Krishna teaches Arjuna that the atman or true self or soul is immortal and is not destroyed, though the body may die. The soul has always existed and will always continue to exist. Krishna speaks: "There never was a time when I, nor thou, nor any of these princes of earth *was not*; nor shall there ever come a time, hereafter, when any of us shall *cease to be* (2:12). These remarks by Krishna stimulate Arjuna into probing more deeply into the nature of life and his place in the cosmos.

There are three points in particular that are discussed. They have to do with the concept of *karma* or moral law and the action prescribed by it through *dharma* or duty, *jnana* knowledge, and *bhakti* devotion. *Karma* is the belief that every action carries with it certain moral consequences which attach themselves to the actor, resulting in reward or punishment. It is comparable to the moral law of cause and effect, and the Judeo-Christian maxim of "What you sow, so shall you reap." *Dharma* is the duties associated with being in a particular caste. The word *dharma* is derived from the root *dhri*, meaning "to support." *Dharma* or the law is what supports the universe. "Those who know and perform without resistance their own *Dharma* (*svadharma*), the duties imposed on them by the circumstances of their birth, become themselves a support, a well-functioning organ, of the universal being" (Campbell *Wild Gander* 174-75). When *dharma* is done properly, the affect is to acquire good karma. This results in the participants being reborn into a higher caste in their next life, until union with God is reached.

Arjuna says: "O Krishna now that I behold the faces and forms of my kindred and loved ones, thus arrayed against each other, and chafing for the fight, my heart faileth me. My legs tremble; mine arms refuse to do my bidding" (1:27-29). As Arjuna is of the warrior caste, it is his duty to act as a warrior. If he displays cowardice, then he will not go to heaven. Krishna reminds him that it is better to do his own duty than to do the duty of another, regardless of how well he does another's duty. He must be true to his own station in life. Krishna speaks: "This folly and unmanly weakness is most disgraceful, contrary to thy duty—such weakeneth the foundation of honor" (2:2) Those remaining faithful to their designated duties will reap good karma, thereby, enabling them to proceed through the cycle of *samsara* more rapidly. *Samsara* is the causal chain of repeated births, old ages, deaths, and rebirths. Some people believe this cycle can be broken by honoring the duties of their caste. The end of *samsara* is known as *moksha* or release from the cycle. It is a form of liberation.

Arjuna grew up in a caste system and would well appreciate and understand this notion of social duty and service. His was not to question it, but to honor it through action. Those raised in the West would be less likely to adhere to such a concept, as individuality and self-expression is stressed over social identity. However, the Hindu's believe that honoring their *dharma* is a way to get closer to God, so their social structure becomes a catalyst for individual spirituality. This implies that salvation is open to everyone. Westerners would be less quick to observe social constraints; however, for Arjuna, loss of individuality is not the question, but whether his actions are right or wrong. Arjuna wonders whether it would be better to lay down his arms and practice a life of austerity and asceticism, so that liberation will be gained by way of non-action.

However, Krishna tells him that even those who meditate still need to breathe and eat, so total non-action is impossible. The answer is to give up the fruits of action which lead to rebirth. This is done by not being attached to the consequences of action, but by doing action in a sort of disinterested way, simply because it is proper, not because it is good or evil. This is similar to the idea of "disinterested piety" found in the Biblical account of Job. Job worships God not to receive reward or escape punishment, but because it is the right thing to do. It is desire, not action, which chains people to the cycle of rebirth. Krishna speaks: "Do thy best, according to the dictates of thy Duty, and then maintain that equal-mindedness which is the mark of the Yogi. He who hath attained the Yogi consciousness is able to rise above good and evil results" (2:48, 50).

Bhakti is the path of love or devotion to God, often conceived as a personal experience by way of hymns and prayers, rather than by way of rituals and sacrifices. *Bhakti* devotion is another lesson for Arjuna, who learns that those who concentrate on a personal God (Krishna) wholeheartedly are truly on their way to being united with the impersonal God (Brahman). Joseph Campbell wrote that *Bhakti* yoga "consists in giving one's life wholly in selfless devotion to some beloved being or thing, who becomes, thereby, in fact, one's 'chosen god'" (*Myths to Live By* 100). Campbell points out that Paul Tillich would view this object of veneration as one's "ultimate concern." This devotional love of Arjuna for his God Krishna is like the love expressed by the disciples of Christ. In both Arjuna's case and the devotees of Christ, they were able to talk directly with the divine one and even argue points of interest (*Ibid* 155-56). However, it requires more than the emotional to enter completely into God; it also involves practical applications, as is implied with *karma* and *dharma*, and the intellectual supplied by *jnana* yoga.

Jnana yoga or knowledge concerns itself with disciplining the mind and being able to discriminate the images which arise as a result of sensory input. Interestingly, the five Pandu princes personify the five physical senses. Thus, the battle which takes place in the *Gita* is not a battle on earth, but one within the mind and heart of Arjuna. Krishna tells Arjuna:

> The man who allows his mind to dwell closely on the objects of sense, becomes so wrapped up in the object of his contemplation that he cre-

ated an attachment which binds him to them. But he who hath gained freedom from attachment to, or fear of, objects of sense; he who findeth his strength and love in the Real Self: he gaineth Peace (2:62, 64).

Meditation lets the interested learn to understand the thoughts, direct the feelings, and become detached from the fruits of their actions. Those who meditate observe the stuff of the mind, seeing when it comes into existence, knowing why it stays, and how and when it departs. Arjuna learns to discriminate between *maya* or illusion, and that which is eternal and of Brahman, the Supreme God. This meditational discernment is accompanied by a peace attained from eventually mastering the senses.

The *Gita* is a primary source on yoga philosophy of which *karma*, *bhakti*, and *jnana* are three of its faces. I have discussed what each of these is separately and wish now to address how they work jointly. It is interesting that Campbell believed that yoga may provide "a master key to the inward dimensions of *all* symbolic forms" (Mythic Image 278).

Yoga comes from the word "*yug*" which means to yoke or join together. This means to concentrate and direct attention to disciplines and practices which foster the union of the soul (atman) with the Spirit (Brahman), as this is the essential goal of yoga. Krishna said: "Freedom from pain and sorrow, is known by the name of Yoga, which means Spiritual Union" (6:23).

Arjuna learns that yoga incorporates an attitude of detachment, freeing him from karmic action. The motive for action becomes focused on service to the Real Self regardless of the appearance the action manifests in the illusory world. Arjuna would no longer judge whether something is good or evil, but whether it serves the Real Self. Only those who transcend the illusory world of opposites are free to act without the attachment of *karmic* consequences. Aurobindo wrote that Arjuna must "look with equal eyes; receive with an equal heart and mind all that comes to him; friend and ally, opponent and enemy. Observe all with the deep regard of the impersonal spirit" (520). This is like a man who has a dream and while he sleeps he witnesses his body soaring high above the earth. He looks back at it and observes the blue and white sphere floating in a sea of blackness. As he looks upon the planet, he notices how still it is, quiet, serene, without borders, without politics, without religions or governments. At this moment, he realizes that there is no separation or division on his planet. As he begins to descend back to his world, he begins to hear the murmurings of its inhabitants and how they bicker with one another. They discuss their differences and why they are better than others. The dreamer suddenly awakes knowing that the differences in the world and the problems that have resulted are the result of ignorance. Those who do not see from the vantage point of the eternal, dwell in misery, because they believe in the illusion of duality.

Ken Wilber writes that Coomaraswamy said:

> 'Once upon a time,' which begins all fairy tales, is really 'Once beyond time,' and the tale which follows is of a world which temporarily suspends space and time, where play rules supreme and anything is possible. And inasmuch as the real world is no-boundary, the language and imagery of mythology is really much closer to that reality than is linear logic and abstract thinking. Mythology begins to transcend boundaries—boundaries of space and time and opposites in general—and for that reason alone, mythological awareness is one step closer to the real world of suchness (*No Boundary* 126).

In addition to mastery over *karma*, is the *bhakti* yoga attitude of devotion to the Supreme Being. True devotion is more than the observance of ritual and legal doctrine. Jesus taught that the spirit of the law is more vital than the letter of the law. The devotees develop a close intimate rapport with the one who is venerated, this one being the Supreme Being in the form of a person. Thus the incarnation of Vishnu in the form of the god-person, Krishna, to whom Arjuna can communicate. Gandhi wrote that *bhakti* is the "perfection of humility and service of all that lives, the extinction of all 'otherness' and ill-will, and contentment in willing surrender" (Desai 87).

Arjuna learns throughout his dialogue with Krishna that he is part of the immutable, immortal, self-existing creatureliness of the universe. His true self, the atman, is indestructible, and is, in essence, of and in the divine. Krishna tells Arjuna:

> I am the Spirit which is well-seated in the consciousness of all beings, the reflection of which they each know as 'I,' or the Ego (10:20).
>
> I am That which is the essential principle in the seed of all beings and things in nature; and everything whether animate or inanimate is infilled with me—without Me nothing could exist for even the twinkling of an eye. Every being or thing that can be known is the product of an infinitesimal portion of my power and glory (10:39, 41).

Campbell has a pleasant passage in *The Flight of the Wild Gander* that reads:

> I am not my body, my feelings, my thoughts, but the consciousness of which these are the manifestations. For humans are, in every particle of their being, precipitations of consciousness; as are, likewise, the animals and plants, metals cleaving to a magnet and waters tiding to the moon. And as the great physicist, Erwin Schrödinger, states in his book, *My View of the World*: 'To divide or multiply consciousness is something meaningless. In all the world, there is no kind of framework within which people can find consciousness in the plural; this is simply something they construct because of the spatio-temporal plurality of individuals, but it is a false conception. What, he asks, justifies you in obstinately discovering this difference—the difference between you and someone else—when objectively what is there is *the same*? This life of yours which you are living is not merely a piece of the entire existence, but is in a certain sense the *whole*; only this whole is not so constituted that it can be surveyed in one single glance. And this, as people know, is what the Brahmins express in that sacred, mystic formula which is really so simple and so clear: *Tat tvam asi*, this is you. Or, again, in such words as 'I am in the east and in the west, I am below and above, I am this whole world' (197).

The *Bhagavad Gita* is an unusual example of a myth because it is a philosophical-spiritual discourse on the nature of things. Arjuna's journey is less in story form and more in dialogue form. Wilber writes that mythological language is "associative and integrative," therefore, it is a clear and true reflection of the physical reality of the universe. He speaks about myth's mutual "interdependence and interpenetration of all things and events." Myths are the stories that provide insights about the fundamental nature of the universe. They speak about humankind's universality, and point to their "fundamentally joyous unity with all of creation, a wholeness that whisks people far beyond the dismally petty affairs of day-to-day routine and plunges them into the vast and magical world of the transpersonal" (*Spectrum* 270).

Arjuna and Krishna are actually personifications of the same being, meaning the author's psyche, revealing unconscious processes about the author's perception of reality. The *Gita* writings are closely connected with the unconscious as the symbols comprising the story are less camouflaged than in most myths. The language that the author uses has a rational component to it as if he is writing to clarify the metaphors of his mind. Arjuna's journey is an implied battle, his army against another army. The real battle which takes place throughout the *Gita* is Arjuna's struggle between the emotions and the intellect. He consciously makes an effort to discriminate between his passion and his reason. Arjuna's projection is onto Krishna, the portion of his psyche which has not been flooded by consciousness. Arjuna is consciousness questioning Krishna, the unconscious. The descriptions that Krishna supplies Arjuna with are full of symbols, and yet, these symbols are continuously reinforced throughout the myth. Most myths have a beginning and move towards a point of completion, whereas each chapter in the *Gita* is complete in itself. Ideas are reinforced and new ones are introduced; however, they all direct themselves towards the same end, knowing Brahman. This end is not only implied in symbols, but also in discourse.

Arjuna is a great hero because he slays the dragons, demons, and warriors of his psyche, as well as makes friends with them. His tale is not about combat in the outer world, but about knowing himself so that he will understand how to participate in the outer world. There is no deceptive message in this tale, for it is written clearly on each page: Atman and Brahman are one; know yourself and know God.

Arjuna's call to adventure, his departure occurs when he is faced with fighting his own kinsmen. These are people he has known for years and are part of his bloodline. Arjuna must decide between retreating from the fight or do his duty and kill his relatives. This leads him to question whether his being faithful to his duty or *dharma* is right or wrong. He is willing to sacrifice honor, family ties, and social acceptance for the sake of following the voice within. This is the beginning of his spiritual adventure. Had Arjuna gone directly into battle without stopping to ask whether it is right to kill his kinsmen, he would never have met the god Krishna and learned the inner doctrine supplied by his unconscious. Arjuna, unlike the heroes Gilgamesh, Owein, and Luke Skywalker, is not interested in glory, fame, or adventure. He is content to see his kinfolk unite and make peace. This places Arjuna ahead of the other heroes being investigated in this thesis. He is already physically well developed and accomplished as a champion warrior and archer. Arjuna's call to adventure begins at the second stage as an intellectual inquiry, motivated by compassion for others.

The initiation stage of Arjuna's journey is his initial refusal, or perhaps I might call it hesitation, to join the fighting. Arjuna is unable to fight because he has directed all his energy to the question at hand: Is it right action to kill my own kin? Arjuna sits with Krishna in the middle of two opposing armies; like his decision, he must choose between two opposing ideas. Arjuna will not make a decision until he has heard Krishna speak his thoughts. Arjuna's trials and encounters with the powerful forces of life all lie within himself, his psyche. There is never a mention of any worldly object which he must face, other than the concept of certain emotional challenges. Arjuna must face the opposing army; yet, he is not afraid to die, but to kill, and herein lies his emotional challenge. The war acts as a catalyst to Arjuna's spiritual inquiry. Had his life been one without conflict, Arjuna would most aptly have never stopped to question what a meaningful existence is and how he is to live it.

Arjuna does return to performing his duty as a warrior, but now he does so knowing why he fights and where to direct his heart, not to any person or social custom, but to the Supreme Being. The social custom is simply a medium for the performance of right action. The boon Arjuna returns with is the knowledge of the inner doctrine, the Supreme bliss which comes with knowing the Real Self.

The shadow force in this myth is surprisingly weak, as far as being personified in a particular character, while it is predominant in most myths. This is another example of the "second stage" journey. The Kauravas who are to fight the Pandus are viewed by Arjuna as his kin, thus his projection onto them lacks some of the intensity the shadow demands in other myths. Therefore, the Kauravas cannot serve for the total projection of the psyche's dark side. Arjuna learns from Krishna that the "powers of aggression and egotism" to be defeated are within himself (Harding *Psychic Energy* 115-16). Arjuna's insights are in part due to his sophistication and psychological maturity. He has had many years in exile to reason on his situation, and perhaps he has reconciled some of the malicious feelings he might have toward an enemy. This is partially a result of his yogic attitude on right action, knowing that revenge is not an answer to solving life's ordeals. Rather than acting from hatred toward the Kauravas, he struggles with the shadow elements within himself. With the aid of Krishna, he gradually becomes aware that his soul is where the battle needs to be fought. Had Arjuna entered the battle, vengefully, his animosity could have festered. As it was, he reasoned on his fate and thus kept the dragon pacified. Harding wrote regarding the projected evil of which Arjuna was unconscious that "in his anger and resentment towards that evil he separates himself from unconscious identification with the group and at long last comes to recognize that it is his own evil that he has been fighting" (*Ibid* 116).

The anima archetype is personified in the character of Krishna. Indeed, Krishna is a man, and yet, he embodies the elements of the female principle: compassion, liberation, passiveness, and nurturance. He is a figure that Arjuna can love, not romantically, but as one who provides for his well-being. A mother is typically one who fulfills this role. Krishna is the maternal figure who watches over Arjuna and counsels with him at his most dire moments.

Arjuna is the animus archetype, the one who embodies the masculine principles. He is rational, virtuous, and a superior fighter, excelling in archery. The other warriors are indeed animus-like, but in this tale, are not appreciated for their bravery. This is a tale about the mind, and mental victories. Thus the physical events are minimized, while the spiritual are maximized. Arjuna can do all of the physical heroic feats, but is a pilgrim on the spiritual path, who is not mesmerized by worldly delights. Unlike the heroes of the other myths being examined, Arjuna has passed rapidly into the spiritual domain. He does not suffer the travesties of physical trials, but instead, collides with the will of the spirit. In fact, the name "Arjuna" means "one who makes sincere efforts" (Rama 4).

The self archetype is undoubtedly Krishna, whose name means "the center of consciousness" (Rama 4). In chapter eleven Krishna reveals himself to Arjuna in all of his forms. Krishna says: "Behold as a Unity, standing within My body, the whole Universe, animate and inanimate, and all these things else that thy mind impelleth thee to see" (11:7). The self archetype is the all in the All, and the organizer of all the diverse elements of being. Krishna is the incarnation of the All and through philosophical and psychological discourse provides Arjuna with a way to enter his own center and bring order to its opposing tendencies.

Chapter Six
Owein

Owein, also known as *The Lady of the Fountain*, is the third story of the Arthurian legends, written in Welsh, found in the late thirteenth century and believed to be adaptations of Continental romances, the Breton *conte* (Loomis 29). The *Owein* version used in this analysis is contained in *The Mabinogion*, an accumulation of eleven medieval Welsh tales contained in two sources: *The White Book of Rhydderch* (1300-1325) and *The Red Book of Hergest* (1375-1425). *The Mabinogion* is the name given to these tales by their English translator Lady Charlotte Guest (1812-95), whose translation I am using for this thesis. These tales may have their origins in the eleventh century. It is suspected that they were transmitted orally and later written down. They reflect ancient Celtic mythological motifs and folk customs. Owein, like Gilgamesh, is a semi-historical figure, as are characters in the *Owein* story. The setting and influence of the story is that of Norman-French romances. The transformation of the storm into a lovely spring day, the fairy-like qualities of Lunet and the Lady, and the ugly herdsman, indicate that *Owein* is probably of Celtic origin. And the appearance of the lion most likely derives from Androcles (Frappier 116). They represent the late medieval period in Arthurian tradition, and find a parallel with the French teller of tales Chrétien de Troyes. Chrétien's version is called *Yvain: The Knight of the Lion*. Matthews hypothesizes that Chrétien's text emphasizes the rationale behind "Otherwordly happenings," while the *Mabinogion* testifies to the impact these Otherwordly affairs have on the "earthly realm" (8).

It is the knights of this tale who act for Arthur, and he becomes more of an Amherawdyr (Emperor) (Ellis 26-28).

Medieval literature portrays Arthur as a great warrior, skilled knight, and one who expresses nobility and graciousness. It is not surprising then that his knights attach themselves to him with fierce devotion (Guest 31). These tellers of Arthurian legends inherited themes about wastelands, sickly kings, dishonored maidens, and mislead knights. The themes of courtly romance, chivalric adventure, and the king's empowerment by Sovereignty (the Goddess of the Land) composed these quests (Matthews ix).

The tale begins with Arthur holding court at Caerlleon upon Usk. Several of his knights, one being Owein, the son of Uryen, engage in conversation, while Gwenhwyvar sews near the window. Arthur reposes, like Utnapishtim, on a fine silk pillow, and tells his guests that he will sleep before taking his meal. Cynon, a knight, is chosen to tell his most wonderous adventure to the other two knights, Cai and Owein. Cynon begins his tale telling how he was an only child, thinking himself to be great in valour and unbeatable. He won all challenges in his own land and went off then to the farthest regions of the earth in search of more opportunities to become famous.

Cynon describes how his recent travels bring him to a fort by the sea, where two yellow-haired youths accompany him inside. Upon entering the fort, Cynon sees twenty four incredibly beautiful maidens weaving silk. They rise to greet him and remove his armour, wash his clothes and adorn him in new attire. These maidens help make him feel very comfortable, but never speak to him. Cynon tells one of the men there that he wonders whether "anyone can overcome him or if he can overcome everyone." Hence, he seeks adventures to make him famous and test his strength. The man informs Cynon about a quest he may go on for just such an adventure by following a path through the woods that leads to a large, ugly black man, twice the height of any ordinary man, who has one foot and one eye. He is the caretaker of the woods, (like Humbaba in *Gilgamesh*), and has sovereignty over the wild animals. Cynon's encounter with this extraordinary character is surprisingly friendly. This cyclops informs Cynon of the road to take for his adventure. He is told to go to the top of a hill and look into the middle of a valley for a giant green tree. Like Arthur, who rests on his silk pillow in the middle of the room, so too is the tree located in the middle of the valley. Cynon goes to the tree, where he sees a fountain with a marble slab next to it with a silver bowl chained to it. He picks up the bowl and pours water from it onto the slab. At the moment he does this, a large thunder and hail storm follows in which all the leaves of the tree are blown off. When Cynon believes that he can no longer endure the mighty storm, it suddenly clears, bringing with it a beautiful day and a tree filled with the melodious sounds of singing birds. Now come the groans and appearance of a great Black Knight who rides upon a black horse. The Black Knight tells him that the storm killed every person and animal caught outside when it came. Thus, he rides ferociously at Cynon, who readies himself for combat, only to find that he is no match for the Black Knight, who hits him with his lance, and throws him from his horse. The Black Knight takes Cynon's horse and leaves him to walk back to Arthur's court.

On his return to the fort of the yellow-haired people, Cynon meets again the cyclops, who mockingly derides him. To his surprise, the yellow-haired people say nothing of his misadventure and treat him as marvelously as before. This completes Cynon's tale, to which Owein had listened attentively.

The following day, Owein sets out to find the Fountain and encounter the Black Knight. The events leading to Owein's encounter with the Black Knight are the same in detail as were Cynon's, except for his perception and response to them. Owein is even more impressed with the people he meets and places he goes to than was Cynon. Owein and the Black Knight engage in a confrontation, destroying each other's lance and shield, and then strike their deadly blows by sword. Owein gets the best of the Black Knight and inflicts a mortal wound to his head. The Knight turns away and flees on his horse back to his castle with Owein in hot pursuit. The Black Knight barely makes it through the two gates, while Owein finds himself in dire straits, as one gate falls on his horse, cutting it in two pieces. A moment later, another gate falls in front of Owein, thus trapping him. A yellow-haired maiden, named Lunet, suddenly appears and helps Owein to escape by giving him a magic ring to wear and a stone to clasp in his hand making him invisible. He escapes to her chamber where she takes care of him and feeds him. The room is as lavishly decorated as was the fort of the yellow-haired people.

Soon afterwards, the Black Knight dies and the people of his domain mourn. Owein observes the Black Knight's widow grieving agonizingly, and he falls helplessly in love with her. She is the Lady of the Fountain, also yellow-haired. Lunet convinces the Lady to marry the man who is a better defender of the Fountain than was her husband. The lady tells Lunet that only a knight from Arthur's court could do the task. Lunet tells the Lady that she will travel to Arthur's court and return with such a knight. In fact, Lunet does not travel anywhere, but appears days later, with Owein, under the pretense of having made such a journey. As none of the men of the Lady's court will risk being the protector of the Fountain, they agree that she must marry Owein, who appears to them in all his splendor.

Owein is an heroic and impervious foe to all those who oppose him, and honorably guards the Fountain for three years, much to the pleasure of the people in his domain. Meanwhile, Emperor Arthur has grown sad at not knowing the whereabouts of Owein, and wonders what has become of him. Arthur sets out with three thousand men to find Owein, and they travel onwards to the Fountain where Arthur's knights confront the new Black Knight, not knowing that he is Owein. Owein defeats them without fail, and finally Gwalchmai, Arthur's finest knight, confronts Owein. The two battle for days until Gwalchmai's helmet is knocked off and Owein recognizes him as his cousin. Arthur declares the confrontation a draw.

Owein now asks his Lady to acquiesce to his plan to travel with Arthur to the Isle of Britain for three months, and then return home to her. She reluctantly agrees. However, Owein stays away for three years, and thus is denounced one day while eating at Arthur's court by Lunet who removes his ring because of his failure to return to his Lady. Owein feels terrible and departs the following day to the outermost regions of the world, where he becomes wild like the animals, roaming and grazing like they do. This is much the way Gilgamesh behaved after the death of Enkidu, who likewise originally behaved like the animals.

Owein comes to a park owned by a widowed Countess who helps him to recover just in time for him to confront an evil earl who wishes to take away all the Countess's remaining possessions. After Owein saves the Countess's land and treasures, he continues on his journey to the remotest places. Owein witnesses a lion and a serpent fighting each other, and the lion getting the worst of it. Owein intervenes, killing the serpent, and with that the lion becomes his companion following him wherever he travels. While relaxing around their campfire, they hear sounds. It is Lunet, who has been imprisoned in a stone wall because Owein did not return to the Lady of the Fountain. If he does not appear soon and set her free, she is to be killed. While Owein decides what to do about Lunet, he meets an earl who feeds him well and tells him about his two sons who are being held by a giant who will kill them unless the earl gives him his daughter. Owein, with the assistance of the lion, who fights better than Owein, kills the giant. Later, Owein meets two youths who are about to burn Lunet. He and the lion fight the youths to their deaths. In each of these battles, Owein locked the lion up so as to make the fight more equal, and both times the lion escaped to aid the still weak Owein. Owein returns to the Lady of the Fountain, reconciles himself to her, and brings her with him to Arthur's court, where she lives as his wife.

Another version adds that Owein continues his quest and fights the Black Oppressor who has slain the husbands of twenty four women and keeps them imprisoned. Owein has the Black Oppressor at a disadvantage, and thus the Black Oppressor pleads with Owein to spare him his life in return for his being one who will turn his house into a place to support the weak and the strong. Owein agrees and then takes the women to Arthur's court. He lives there for awhile and then continues to travel abroad.

Owein begins his first cycle and departure when he hears the story about the Fountain. It awakens his desires for knightly pursuits and praises. Owein decides that he must encounter the Black Knight and vanquish him. He knows that this will make him famous. All heroes want to be better than everyone else, standing apart from the rest. The only way that they can achieve this is to do something that no one else has done. Thus, they tend to do that which is new and different or do it better than the last time it was done. All heroic victories begin as physical conquests over others and later, if the victors continue to grow, as spiritual victories over themselves. Whether they are aware of it or not, mythic participants integrate their unconscious into their Self, and thus they reach greater completion. It is notable that the great hero Arthur wakes after the tale has been told. Cynon's tale may be a personification of Arthur's dreamworld. Arthur becomes the Sleeping Lord (Matthews 108) who, like the sleeping god Vishnu, creates the world while dreaming. Arthur has already completed such a journey, and has become the locus of power for his knights to do the same.

Owein's initiation begins when he repeats the journey told to him by Cynon. He meets the giant cyclops, known as a "bachlach," the herder of animals who carries a club, and follows his directions to the Fountain where he fights and defeats the Black Knight. By this victory he defeats the champion of that realm, which no one has done prior to Owein. This begins his succession of victories over the physical world. Owein is awarded for this first stage when he marries the Lady of the Fountain and becomes protector of the land. Incidentally, the boundary of the Black Knight's domain (later the Lady's domain) is faraway and accessible to Owein only after the encounter with the Black Knight who is summoned by the magical fountain. "This boundary marks the entrance to the 'other world' of the psyche" (Bryce 83). Owein becomes the new guardian of the enchanted world.

The first cycle's round of adventure ends when Owein is recognized by Arthur and the other knights as a new champion and protector of the Fountain. Owein returns as a champion of the world, and like Gilgamesh, is not yet ready to play the role of husband and landlord. Gilgamesh was king and it was his duty to be a good ruler to his people, which he was not. Owein's duty is to his Lady and their kingdom. Both Gilgamesh and Owein think that the right thing to do is to slay dragons. Gilgamesh can never settle for being normal and ignores the advice of the barmaid Siduri to enjoy life. Owein ignores the advice of his wife to stay at home and goes off with Arthur. Both need to experience a traumatic event before they will awaken to their shortsightedness. Owein has found his bliss, namely his beautiful wife and being Lord of a kingdom. But now Arthur reappears as a reminder of his worldly duties. The conflict Owein faces is a spiritual problem: how to be true to himself and also responsible to his Lady (Campbell *Transformations* 237).

The second cycle and its departure is introduced to Owein when a messenger enters Arthur's court and denounces Owein in front of everyone for not keeping his promise to the Lady to return to her after three years of roaming around with the other knights. Owein is still a little boy who enjoys playing games with the other little boys. The winner is the one who slays the biggest and most terrible monster. It never dawns on Owein that responsibility and honor to his Lady may require discipline and courage beyond that of facing any monster. Some adults like to remain Peter Pans, acting like little children who do not have to grow up. Becoming an adult brings with it responsibility to other people. Grownups are no longer free to do anything that they like, but must consider others before taking action. It is apparent from Owein's forgetfulness, that he has a wife and is the guardian of a kingdom, that his sojourn has been "Otherwordly" (Matthews 113).

Owein is initiated a second time, much in the way that Gilgamesh was initiated. Owein feels terrible and ashamed and leaves Arthur's court to roam the woods. He looks and smells awful, lives off of the land, and loses most traces of his humanness. This is his (to use Jung's term) enantiodromia, where he hits bottom and has no place to go except to die or to begin the long climb up. The various people that he meets while in his animal state of consciousness stir him to recover his human consciousness. In this second round of adventures, Owein continues to slay monsters, yet not for glory, but to be a champion of the weak and oppressed. He saves a lion, rescues

Lunet, helps out a Countess, saves young maidens from the castle of Evil. He is on the road to becoming responsible and acting with conscious intention. Owein's period of madness actually leaves him healed. He reintegrates the primal elements of his psyche stimulated by his living amongst the plants and animals. He is truly transformed, having become the master of the Otherworld in the guise of the Black Knight, and master of the earthly realm as the new Wild Herdsman (Matthews 114-115), able to tame the beasts, especially the lion. He plays the hospitable host to Arthur as did the Yellow-haired Man to him. And Owein helps to transform the Black Oppressor into one who will be an hospitable host for wayfarers (*Ibid* 128). There is a powerful cyclical theme in this tale with the old continuously making way for the new.

The second return for Owein casts him in the role of one who has grown up. He has realized his heroic pursuits for what they are and appreciates them. Now he reconciles himself to the Lady and returns to live with her. He is not a highly developed character spiritually, but at least he is a responsible human being with some spiritual actualization.

Owein is the quest of an individual who proceeds beyond the boundaries of normal life. "The profound interpretation of such a tale is of the human soul in search of the Spirit" (Bryce 9). The unification of the soul with the Spirit is cultivated by the emergence of the archetypes. The shadow is a dominant archetype in myths as it is the dark side that must be reconciled in order to become psychically balanced. When the shadow first makes its appearance, it is treated as the enemy and attacked. It is later that the shadow is recognized as a fundamental part of human nature. The shadow can no more be destroyed than can one side of a coin be eliminated without simultaneously destroying it entirely. A magnet is a magnet because it has a negative and a positive pole. If either pole is eliminated then the magnet ceases to have form. Likewise, the shadow has a dark side and a good side. The hero needs to tame the dark side and to identify with the good side. Owein tries to destroy the dark side by conquering the Black Knight, thus throwing the land into chaos. This is the same phenomenon which occurred when Gilgamesh and Enkidu slew

Humbaba and tilted the balance of nature. When Owein uses the energies of the shadow to free Lunet and overthrow the man who is taking over the Countess's domain, he is expressing the good side of his shadow. In other words he is using its energies to assist life, rather than to promote the senseless destruction of it. A further example of the shadow is found at the fort of the Yellow-haired man and twenty four maidens. And at the fort of the Black Oppressor with his twenty four captive maidens. The Yellow-haired people are really fairies, with magical powers. They live in a palace of power from which visiting knights are rejuvenated to make ready for their quest. The maidens do not speak because they are images from the psyche which bring healing and consoling. These maidens attire Owein in new garments, hence, they make one new again. This is the good side of these shadow figures. When oppressed, their energies, far from rejuvenating, must themselves be given life. The Black Oppressor's kingdom is the antithesis of the yellow-haired man. One is the result of what happens when psychic energies are allowed to integrate with consciousness, the other is the wasteland which results from their suppression. These two realms mirror each other. One being symbolic of the radiant psyche that has welcomed all those who seek entrance, the other shrouded in darkness because of its inhospitable ways.

These are the "forest years" where real psychological integration takes place. Even though Owein trudges through the muck and mire of despair, he is moved by the tragic conditions of others. His empathy and compassion for their plights enable him to pull himself up by his own bootstraps, saving himself spiritually, while others physically. It is from this low point in his life that he redeems himself from shame and worthlessness by his heroic and noble acts to those who find themselves in dire straits. It is by no coincidence that his faithful companion in these later adventures is the lion, who symbolizes courage and nobility. Owein will need courage of a new sort, not to fight wrongdoers, but to make good on his promise to return to what implies a somewhat sedentary lifestyle. Sedentary in the physical sense but not necessarily in the spiritual.

Owein, like Aeneas, is a traveler in a foreign land who needs to be hidden from its dangers. Owein receives a magic ring making him invisible, Aeneas has a cloud thrown over him by Venus. Both Dido and the Lady have intermediaries who convince them to marry this newcomer. The Fountain is a storm-making spring. The Yellow-haired people are sun deities. Owein defeats the Black Knight, an earth deity and yet becomes one himself, while at the same time being wed in a yellow coat of satin, the color of the sun (Loomis 71). This is a struggle between the old storm god and the new sun god. The young god succeeds to the old god's privileges (Loomis 71), hence a theme of fertility. These ritualistic elements were commonly reflected in magic-sacral rites to rejuvenate the kingdom's powers, as the old king is sacrificed and replaced by one who is youthful and vigorous, thus reenacting Nature's cycle of birth, death, and regeneration (Edmunds 29).

The anima in this myth is worn by both the Lady of the Fountain and Lunet, whose name means "little moon" (Guyer 93). Lunet is the unselfish friend whose motives can only be guessed. She does not seem to gain anything from her bringing together Owein and the Lady. In fact, she is punished because Owein betrays the Lady and Lunet is blamed for having introduced them. She is truly Owein's feminine side, the helper who appears out of nowhere at the most perilous moments, and at her most perilous moment it is Owein who comes out of nowhere to her rescue. Both need each other to make their lives more complete. The lady is the typical anima type seen in myths. She is the lover of the hero, the person to whom his anima has been projected onto with ferocious intensity. He is bedazzled by her beauty and she is attracted to his knightly skills. However, as is usually the case with projections, that which pleased the Lady about Owein is what also separates them. Projection is self-centered and selfish, concerned only with its own satisfaction. It is the philosophy of hedonism. When the projection wears off, the two people are left with the "real" each other and if they can manage still to be in love, then the relationship will endure. The moment the Phantom of the Opera's mask is removed, the viewers discover whether the Lady can love him as he really is. When Owein's projected anima falls from his Lady, he is back to chasing dragons again. It is his heroic feats of courage and strength that the Lady admires and that also cause her to be angry at Owein when he leaves her to do more of the same. The Lady of the Fountain has no generic name, but is referred to as Lady. This implies the universality of her character as not being a real person, but a mythological one. She is the Earth Mother who controls the primal chaos in the guise of the storm-producing fountain. She represents a fairy tale world and not the real world. One is reminded of Dido in the *Aeneid*, who tries desperately to keep Aeneas from taking leave of her and in her mourning for his absence turns her love into hate for him. She curses Aeneas and then takes her own life. The lady, likewise, denounces Owein, but later is reconciled to him. Like Dido, the Lady does not remain faithful to her late husband, but even before meeting this newcomer in her life decides to marry this new champion. The Lady has a strong sense of duty to have her Fountain and homelands protected. In fact, the Lady speaks of the Fountain as her own, showing her maternal attachment to It. This underscores the notion of the Fountain as having generative powers (Heffernan 115). The women in Owein's life protect him as a mother would protect her child from harm. These women reinforce the idea that the anima in this tale has several sides to it.

When reading these myths with their like tales of man meets woman, hero meets princess, I wonder to what degree the attraction between an Owein and his lady occurs solely at a biological level. This is how I would imagine Freud to interpret such meetings. And he would probably be apprehensive of the entire affair. For he believed that the sexual impulse was a wild boar, whose furry could only destroy those who could not control it. Grant it, sexuality is rooted in biology, however, it does not end there. As Jung recognized, there is another side to this strong drive. This other side is the spiritual, upward moving drive of the psyche. Jung's *coincidentia oppositorum* connected the biological with the spiritual, so that both the horizontal and vertical dimensions could be actualized to their fullest. Freud saw only the biological dimension and this made the human journey a frightful one controlled by irrational forces. Adding additional Jungian light to the understanding of the psyche's processes, now, "sexuality could become the material for transformation, the starting point of a renewal of the personality, provided that individuals recognized its value in connection with the depth of the psyche" (Frey-Rohn 182). These myths do not degenerate into personal sexual romps found so much today on television and movie screens. There are universal, transformative messages within for those who are willing to peer keenly and wonder at these numinous worlds. As Jung pointed out, even the projection that expresses sexually at first, is but an initiator to a whole other encounter. If this were not so, the growth of these mythic heroes would remain constant, and they would be as irrelevant as Hollywood's studs.

The animus figure in this tale's first journey is the Black Knight whom Owein defeats and whose guise he assumes, all outwardly. Bryce writes that "the old king symbolizes an inferior part of the hero himself." This death of an old king signifies the birth of a new way of life in the new king — one who will advance further on his inner journey and development of the Self (84). In the second journey it is the lion, whom Owein saves and integrates as a helpmate. The alchemist Abraham Lambspring wrote: "The Sage says that a wild beast is in the forest, whose skin is of blackest dye. If any man cut off his head, his blackness will disappear, and give place to snowy white." Often myths describe the slaying of the inner beast as being a move towards spiritual completeness. However, if this beast can be tamed and its powers internalized, spiritual development has proceeded a step further (Bryce 47). The lion is an adequate symbol for Owein's transformation as it is "associated with the sun, its affirmative tendencies being equated with royal courage, will, strength, nobility, power, and invincibility, with victory of spirit over matter." In addition, the lion represents "the illumination of the conscious" (Norman 58). Lunet is identified with the moon, the light of night. She, like the lion, is a helper to Owein. Apparently, Owein needs both the consciousness of the dayworld and the unconscious of the nightworld to complete his quest. Owein is the strong gallant fighter of foes and conqueror of evil. He is the brave knight who will rescue the damsel in distress and restore order to a disenchanted land. The animus is strong in Owein. It is what makes him brave and gallant, able to be victorious over the most unspeakable situations. In order for Owein to develop spiritually, his animus must marry his anima. The rough and tough knight and his animus need to unite with the gentle side of his anima. As the knight develops compassion within his own being, he will be able to feel greater empathy towards other people. This quality makes its appearance in Owein after he roams the earth as a wild animal.

The self archetype in this myth does not fall obviously upon any particular person. We can guess that Emperor Arthur is a well balanced person who has undergone the tests and ordeals which his less experienced knights face. The story tells us little about him and he has a seemingly small role to play in Owein's quest. However, Arthur does seem to act as a motivational force for Owein, as he is the one who provides the action for Owein to return to his court. And his kingdom is a place to recuperate since it is the center of the world. It is the power source for the great adventures which take place. Thus Arthur's court is a mandala and through this symbol generates psychic energy. Likewise, the Fountain is a magical place with mana-like powers, and unleashes psychic energy when disturbed, causing chaos, but always returning to a state of rest. The Fountain functions as if it awaits the next being to participate in the integration of the unconscious and consciousness, spirit and matter. The Fountain is a type of "baptismal image" (Heffernan 109). Owein's journey "starts out from a garden setting—this one outside the castle walls of a lord—itself a traditional representation of the perfect state of inward order and serenity which man first had and then lost; it also ends there" (*Ibid* 110). The court of Arthur is likewise a powerful center of psychic energy. Both are places where people come to enter into their own psychological center. Those who come to Arthur's court either do so to recover from difficult times or to prepare themselves for new adventures. The Fountain is the place where the action of the protagonist revolves. Owein goes there to prove himself and he returns there to be reunited with Arthur and the other knights. The Fountain is a magical place of rejuvenation, where a knight goes to be reborn a hero. Even the land is destroyed by a storm and is made new again. The Lady loses a husband and finds a better one. Owein forgets about Arthur for three years and later his wife for three years. A clue that Owein will return to humanity is when he blushes when the Countess sees him (Roberts 178). It is only upon his reconciliation with his wife and return to Arthur, at the end of the tale, that he is able to be husband and knight (*Ibid* 179). Owein is one who has completed his pilgrimage, tamed the Black Knight within himself and has been reconciled to his Lady, thus regaining paradise (Heffernan 119). Owein travels from the earthly paradise of Arthur's court to the Otherworldly paradise of his Lady's kingdom. The union of both realms becomes complete when Owein hands Arthur the sovereignty of the Fountain (Matthews 130), and Owein and his Lady settle in Arthur's kingdom. Both realms are energized through this mutual exchange and integration.

Chapter Seven

Star Wars

Joseph Campbell was interviewed by Bill Moyers for a six-part television series, *The Power of Myth*, filmed at George Lucas's "Skywalker" ranch. In 1985 at the National Arts Club awards banquet honoring Campbell, Lucas, the creator of *Star Wars*, delivered this speech, which well acknowledges his indebtedness to the scholarly work of Campbell.

> About ten years ago I set out to write a children's film, and I had the idea of doing a modern fairy tale. My friends all around said, 'What are you doing? Are you crazy? You have to do something important, something socially relevant, something that is art with a capital A. You have to do what *we* are doing.'
>
> I listened and went forward with my idea anyway, started doing research, started writing. A year went by and I read and wrote many drafts of this work, but something wasn't quite right. And then I stumbled cross *The Hero with a Thousand Faces*, and for the first time I really began to focus. I discovered that I was approaching the same themes intuitively and I began to see a lot of parallels. Then I read *The Flight of the Wild Gander* and got into the *Mask of God* series, and this sense of being on the right track continued to grow. Out of this period of discovery and work came *Star Wars*.
>
> Much later I was given a set of tape-recorded lectures by Joseph, and after listening for hours and hours and hours I said, I've got to meet this man. There is a wonderful life force that comes through the wit and charm of Joe's inspired speech that is as wonderful as the books.
>
> On my birthday about two years ago Joe was in San Francisco and I went to his speaking engagement and ran around afterwards backstage to meet him. Since then I've gotten to know him better. Eventually he came out and stayed with me for a weekend and said, 'Gee, I'd like to see some of your films.' He sat through *Star Wars*, *The Empire Strikes Back*, and *Return of the Jedi*, which no one else had ever done, and he actually came out chipper and wide awake. In fact, he asked, 'Do you have any more?' And I said, 'Sure do,' and I showed him *American Graf-*

fiti and *THX*. We spent the rest of the weekend together just talking. It was one of the finest experiences of my life.

I think you can say about some authors that their work is greater than the personage, but with Joseph, as magnificent as his work is, he's as wonderful, as completely insightful and powerful as his creations. He's a simply wonderful man. To conclude, I can only say: Joe, you've become my Yoda (Stone 8).

The *Star Wars* trilogy by George Lucas consists of the popular movies known as *Star Wars, The Empire Strikes Back*, and *The Return of the Jedi*. These "myths" revolve around the young Luke Skywalker and his struggle for freedom against the evil Empire and the dark side of the Force. The tale unfolds on planet Tatooine where Luke lives with his aunt and uncle, farmers of a sort. Luke is energetic and passionate, eager to join the freedom fighters who seek to crush the Empire before it crushes them. On his desert planet Luke is able to purchase from scavengers two droids who have fled there to avoid capture by the evil Darth Vader. One droid is golden colored known as See-Threepio (C-3PO), who is able to translate six million languages and is programmed for protocol. The other is called Artoo-Detoo (R2-D2), from whom Luke stumbles across a holographic image of princess Leia asking for help from the Jedi knight known as Obi-Wan Kenobe, and who contains the blueprints of the "Death Star," which the Rebels hope to destroy. Even on Luke's home planet, he encounters dangerous Tusken Raiders known as the sandpeople, but is rescued by Obi-Wan Kenobe, who will be Luke's special helper throughout his journey. Luke tells Obi-Wan that he cannot get involved because he has work to do. Obi-Wan says: "That sounds like your uncle talking." And suggests that Luke learn about the Force. While Luke is away from home one day, Imperial warships of the Empire attack his planet and kill his aunt and uncle, leaving Luke with no reason to remain there. Obi-Wan teaches him the way of the Force, thus developing the intuitive skills needed to be a Jedi.

Luke learns about the dark times that the malicious Empire have brought and how Darth Vader was seduced by the dark side of the Force. Luke learns that the Force is a religion; it is an energy field created by all living things, penetrating and surrounding them, while binding the galaxy together. Obi-Wan tells Luke that the Force flows through you; it obeys your commands and controls your actions. Obi-Wan reminds Luke to let go of his conscious intentions and act on instinct, and to reach out with his feelings. Interestingly, Obi-Wan often refers to Luke as a "boy" for he is not yet fully enlightened about his inner self.

Obi-Wan and Luke travel to a spaceport on Tatooine, and enter an alien-packed cantina, a gathering place for riff-raff. Luke sees how Obi-Wan does "mind tricks" on the weak-minded in order to travel the city freely. They meet Han Solo and Chewbacca, who take them in their ultrafast ship to Alderan, a world which is later destroyed by the Death Star.

Luke's mission now requires him to rescue princess Leia from Darth Vader, a leader of the Imperial forces and practitioner of the dark side of the Force. With the help of Han Solo, a vagabond who owes a sizeable debt to Jabba the Hut, and the Wookie Chewbacca, Luke rescues Leia. They finally escape from the Death Star when Obi-Wan sacrifices his material existence, transforming himself into a specter in order for Luke to be free. Obi-Wan's ethereal forces are now free to influence and feed Luke. Luke returns later with the Rebel forces and destroys the Death Star.

The Empire Strikes Back continues as the next part of the *Star Wars* trilogy. The Empire's forces learn the location of the Rebels and land an attack party on the planet Hoth. The Rebels evacuate as many troops as possible while keeping some land and air forces behind for combat. The battle ends with the Rebels' generator being destroyed, but with the Rebel forces escaping. Vader pursues Han, Leia, and Chewbacca in order to lure Luke into a trap, as Vader wants to persuade Luke to join him in ruling the galaxy, harnessing thereby Luke's ability to manipulate the Force.

Meanwhile, Luke is undergoing intense training in the Dagobah planetary system where Yoda lives. Yoda, a little elf-life figure, is nine hundred years of age and master and teacher of Jedi Knights. When Luke first encounters Yoda, Yoda plays the fool in order to discern Luke's disposition, which he concludes is impatient. The spectral figure of Obi-

Wan appears and tells Yoda that we were all impatient and restless once, and to give Luke a chance. Luke improves greatly, but fails the "cave test" when he encounters the dark side of himself and in anger strikes out at whom he believes to be Vader, and learns that it is himself. Luke is told that his friends are in danger, having been captured on a mining planet. Luke, against the advice of Yoda and Obi-Wan, decides to depart to help them, though he is warned that he is not yet ready and could fall into temptation like Vader. Yoda tells Luke that the Force is used for knowledge and defense, never attack: "You must unlearn what you have learned. Try not, do. Illumined beings are we, not this crude matter. Difficult to see, always in motion the future."

Luke reaches the mining colony, knowing that he must face Darth Vader as his ultimate challenge. Han has been put in carbon freeze and taken away by a bounty hunter to Jabba the Hut. Meanwhile, while under attack from enemy gunfire, Leia and Chewbacca, with some help, blast off. Luke fights Vader in a desperate struggle, using all his acquired abilities. Vader gains control and in fact cuts off Luke's hand. Vader informs a startled and incredulous Luke, though he knows in his heart that it is true, that he, Vader, is his father. Vader tries to persuade him to join what would be the most powerful team in the galaxy, but Luke refuses and escapes.

The third part is the *Return of the Jedi*. Luke returns to his home planet with a plan to release Han from the imprisonment of Jabba the Hut. Meanwhile, the Empire is completing a more powerful Death Star and awaits the arrival of the Emperor, who will oversee its progress. Luke's two droids arrive at Jabba the Hut's palace and are led in by Gamorrean pig-like guards to Jabba. The droids tell Jabba that they are a gift from Luke to him, and that Luke, a Jedi Knight will arrive later to bargain for the life of Han.

Leia and Chewbacca have plans similar to Luke's and are partially successful when Leia releases Han from the carbon freeze in which his body has been in hibernation, but are discovered. Luke arrives, only to fall into a pit with a large flesh eating monster, which he slays. However, he remains imprisoned and with his friends faces execution. Luke develops a plan which gets them out of trouble and he destroys Jabba and his debauched companions.

Now, Luke returns to Yoda to continue training, only to see Yoda pass on into another dimension. Obi-Wan tells Luke that Leia is his sister and will one day learn the ways of the Jedi: "A Jedi's strength flows from the Force." Obi-Wan tells him that he cannot escape his destiny.

Luke lands with a small group of ground forces on the Forest Moon of Endor, which is orbited by the new Death Star. His intention is to knock out the generator of the force-field which protects the Death Star. When this is done, fighter planes will attack it and destroy its main reactor. Luke's forces proceed as planned, and Luke goes to the Death Star to confront Vader, his father, in hopes of turning him back to the good side of the Force. The Emperor who is Vader's master, and has been plotting with Vader to overthrow the Rebel Alliance, wants Luke to give into his feelings of anger and hate and thus to join him on the dark side, and be his servant. While Luke moves to victory over Vader and the Emperor, little furry creatures known as Ewoks on the Forest Moon assist the Rebel forces in blowing up the generator, allowing the Rebel fighter ships to attack the Death Star, and emerge victorious.

An important contribution of *Star Wars* is that they are modern myths, written during the late twentieth century and, therefore, are representative of the ideas, passions, conflicts, hopes, and emotional life of people living today. The dramatization of an advanced race of peoples, living in a highly technological world cannot be overlooked, as today, many people, likewise, participate in a world of machines, robots, and computers. Much of the present environment is being destroyed by human beings, motivated by greed and power, using technology as their means to conquer nature. *Star Wars* addresses many of these same issues, albeit through a different scenario, but one which has the same underlying question: Do humans first not have to gain control over their own lives, thoughts, feelings, and the innate forces which move them, before they think they are sufficiently prudent to inform nature how it is to act for them. And each time humans conquer nature, rather than make friends with it, does this not make it easier then to conquer each other, rather than to make friends and work out their own differences? This is why the interaction of the human being with technology needs to be studied in this myth, as well as the psychic interplay of forces at work within Luke, the protagonist.

Such a technological universe intensifies the possibilities for the mythic imagination. The greater the field these energies can be played out in, the greater the likelihood of archetypal connections being made with consciousness. Technology presents new and varied images for the unconscious to reveal itself through. Jung understood the importance of psychological energy. These myths are a battlefield for such energy exchanges. Becoming aware of this energy is what the myths are needed for.

Myths are metaphors "symbolic of spiritual powers within" (Campbell *Open Life* 21), embodying universal ideas on natural or cultural phenomena which are derived from experiences common to all human beings. They are not to be interpreted as literal or factual tales, but as tales that point "beyond facts to something that informs the fact" (*Ibid*). Myths depend upon people's receptivity to them and constitute an attempt to express insights into human nature. They reveal psychological patterns and themes through archetypal and symbolic transformation of people's everyday experiences. These archetypes are composed of objects from nature forming "a vision of the goals of human work" (Frye 113). *Star Wars* is such a myth, a vision quest, a story about heroic figures battling the forces of light and dark, personified through both individual and collective characters, as well as the locales where the story unfolds. *Star Wars* is a metaphorical attempt "to understand and explain the perceived realities of human beings (Villela-Minnerly 387). It "contains valuable clues to people's conscious and unconscious shared values, that is, to the shared wishes, conflicts, and fears of society" (*Ibid* 389).

The symbols in *Star Wars* personify humans as potentially unlimited horizontally and vertically. Horizontally they are very technologically advanced, traveling faster than light around the galaxy in small spacecraft, and have weapons powerful enough to destroy an entire planet with the push of a single button. Vertically those select few who are in communion with their inner world, and "the Force," are semi-divine in power but not necessarily in moral judgment. Luke Skywalker, Obi-Wan Kenobe, and Yoda act as benevolent beings, whereas Darth Vader and the Emperor act as demons. Those who ascend vertically, that it, develop control of the Force, must act morally on the horizontal dimension where their ideas are acted out. They are the ones who ultimately affect the mass consciousness, and must themselves be moral beings in order for the world to remain stable while growing progressively.

Northrop Frye explained that the quest is an aspect of myths. It involves a hazardous journey, an imminent struggle, and recognition of the greatness of the heroic figures by others (186-87). There is a cyclical development to this quest because it is a reflection of nature: the seed that must enter the darkness, struggle, and finally be reborn in its exalted form. An element of the quest is polar opposition between the heroic ones and the enemies of the world. Heroes and heroines are associated with "order, fertility, vigor, and youth" (*Ibid* 188), the enemy with "darkness, confusion, sterility, and old age" (*Ibid* 187-88). Vader and the Emperor use technology for evil and are partially crippled. Obi-Wan says Vader is "more machine now than man — twisted and evil" (*Return of Jedi*). Frye wrote that the victory of this struggle is that of "fertility over the waste land" (193). This victory will come when Luke faces Vader, that is, overcomes the machine.

Luke Skywalker and his Freedom Fighters hazard a journey against Darth Vader and the Empire. Luke first appears as a vital youth with untidy blond hair and white garments signifying his purity and innocence. He spends his time on his Uncle's farm getting ready for the annual harvest. Luke is restless and eager for adventure, gifted, yet having much to learn. Upon acquiring the droids R2-D2 and C-3PO, and witnessing the holographic image which R2-D2 shows of princess Leia, Luke's fascination with this image and the name "Obi-Wan Kenobe" signify the awakening of his latent potential. Luke's loyalty to his friends, and single desire to free his people, though his own life lies in constant peril, are part of his humanity.

When Vader first makes an appearance, he tramples his way in amongst a mass of corpses that his sterile clad soldiers have destroyed with their laser weapons. Vader is hard in appearance, dressed in black armor, emotionally detached from the death at his feet. His soldiers respond to him without reflection upon his commands, as do mindless machines. This image speaks to the audience about a "real fragmentation of the individual even as it is moralized and presented as mythic evil instead" (Rieder 36).

Luke's worlds are covered with water, trees, and marshes signifying the processes of life. Even the deserts he wanders are full of developing life. He often encounters ominous forces and creatures, for nature can be a difficult power to reckon with if the sojourners are not prepared or experienced. Nature, however, is the manifestation of the creative principle in life. When nature's forces are in opposition, the victor ultimately brings forth life. Civilization operates in the same manner, as it "is not merely an imitation of nature, but the process of making a total human form out of nature, and it is impelled by desire" (Frye 105). When Luke undergoes some of his most arduous training under Yoda's guidance, his every encounter with natural forces develops his own self-knowledge and maturity. He also utilizes technology to increase his intuitive skills, as he demonstrates during a practice with his lightsaber. He keeps his eyes covered while reflecting the tiny laser shots that are fired at him by a hovering electronic ball. He learns to focus and direct his desires and his skills through means which will allow others to live life more fully.

Vader spends his time solely on one world, except when destroying others, a planet-machine, a spaceship of destruction, aptly named the "Death Star." This Death Star is an artificial world where life is dead, that is, life exists in or as a machine. I believe the words of Frye apply to Vader's worldview because the images it consists of are "engines of torture, weapons of war, armor, and images of a dead mechanism which, because it does not humanize nature, is unnatural as well as inhuman" (150). Vader's every thought and desire is on how to disrupt the very fabric of civilization, wanting a world of anonymous human machines responsive only to him. Vader lacks empathy for human beings and views them as things to be manipulated, thus their wills and thoughts are inconsequential to him. Vader's life is death through mercilessness and cruelty.

Technology is at an incredibly advanced stage of development, in someways matching the subjective leaps of Skywalker and of Vader. They each use technology in diametrically opposed ways, Luke for the release of life and Vader for its bondage and ultimate extinction. Vader has identified with technology to the point of becoming a partial machine, himself, being hooked up to a life-support system. Vader needs technology for his own survival, and ironically uses it to destroy the lives of others. Luke is not enslaved to the machine and demonstrates that technology is the servant and the human being its director. When luke's hand is cut off and replaced with a mechanical hand to make his body function well again, technology does not determine how he will choose to use his new hand.

A most dramatic moment of the relationship between intuition and technology is when Luke is flying his fightership into a small canal on the Death Star in hopes of firing a blast down a narrow shaft to destroy it. A fighter pilot asks Luke regarding this target, "Are you sure the computer can hit it?" A moment later Luke responds to the ethereal voice of Obi-Wan Kenobe telling him to use the Force. Luke disengages his computer and fires a blast, a direct hit! Luke used a machine to fire the blast, and relied on his intuition to direct the shot. Hence the human and the machine became intuitively united. Interestingly, neither the Force nor computers think; they both operate deductively, that is, they respond to an originative factor, namely, the human being.

The success of Luke Skywalker over himself and the mechanical aspirations of Darth Vader significantly suggest that life consists of a harmonious interchange of naturally and technologically created systems. The abuse of the human intellect and failure to reason on the impressions from life can destroy both life and the people who fail to unite with it. This is why Yoda feared for Luke when he prematurely left his training, before his intuitive skills were fully developed, that he might be swayed to the dark side of the Force. The dark side disrupts people's responses to technology as a malignant tumor disrupts a healthy organism. Incredibly, the droids express more compassion than Vader, because that is the way they were programmed to respond. Vader and the Emperor actually sink below the pre-programmed value systems of these machines. They have so deliberately identified with a mechanized world that is manipulated, programmed, and systematized, that they have lost their own identity. They have become the manipulators, programming other human beings to respond to them as do the unquestioning machines. They disintegrate an entire planet, murdering countless people. This selfish conquest over nature is exemplified by their cold, unfeeling, guiltless nature. What once qualified them as humans is nearly gone.

The *Star Wars* trilogy has the elements of a mother-goddess, father-god system. In fact, it "recapitulates the archetypal pattern of classical myth" (Gordon *Return* 46). Yoda is a chthonic creature who symbolizes the earth and all that is natural. Vader is a sky figure who expresses paternal authority. His name means "Darkfather" and he is the antithesis of Obi-Wan. Vader wants to run the universe with a Death Star which gives not illuminating, but destructive light (Waller 64). The Death Star, Vader's home, unleashes lightning like rays of death down upon one world, and the Emperor even shoots electricity from his hands, symbolic of thunder and lightning. Thus the conflict between matriarchal and patriarchal systems. Vader is unable to balance these two forces and therefore leads himself to doom. Waller wrote: "Lucas has designed a nonanthropocentric universe that has a way of catching off-guard anyone who trusts too completely their own, ego-centric perspective" (*Ibid* 65). And Campbell states, "It's what Goethe said on Faust but which Lucas has dressed in modern idiom—the message that technology is not going to save humanity. Their computers, their tools, their machines are not enough. They have to rely on their intuition, their being true" (*Power of Myth* xiv). The real victors of humanity and technology are not the ones who make discoveries about the world, but about themselves (*Ibid* xiv), and live in such a way that their actions are of redeeming value for society (*Ibid* xv).

Lucas hints that even the most mechanized world cannot escape nature, as when the Skywalker group falls into a garbage pit and encounters an organic life form which feeds on the refuse of machines. Regardless of how advanced technology becomes, there is no elimination of the life which makes technology possible. As Campbell so aptly put it: "The monster masks that are put on people in *Star Wars* represent the real monster-force in the modern world. When the mask of Darth Vader is removed, viewers see an unformed man, one who has not developed as a human individual. He's a bureaucrat, living not in terms of himself, but in terms of an imposed system" (*Power of Myth* 145). An essential question raised by these myths is whether humanity will become subservient to and therefore diminished by the system or whether the system will be used to serve a higher human potential.

In addition to the interaction of human beings with machines, *Star Wars* is a mythological tale about the conflict between good and evil, similar to the Zoroastrian worldview, with Arhura Mazda versus Angra Mainyu. It is also like the *Bhagavad Gita* where a war is fought between families, when in fact the real battle for Arjuna takes place within his soul. This is true for Luke as well. Throughout the movie the audience witnesses the evil Empire trying to crush the Rebel forces who wish only peace and cooperation. The evil Empire is the shadow which wants to crush that part of itself (the Rebels) which denies it unlimited expression. These two opposing armies each have their individual leaders: Luke and Vader.

The myth takes opposing archetypes, creates an entire world for them to be played out in and then reduces them once again to being worn by individuals. *Star Wars* is really the journey of Luke as hero. He is the living archetype who learns to integrate the diversities of his psyche on his journey towards becoming complete.

A particularly exciting point about the *Star Wars'* myths are that they take place in outer space. Space is dark, appearing empty, at least for vast distances, and therefore a naturally nebulous setting for myths to unfold. In reality, these myths do not occur in outer space but inner space. They are really about the unconscious and its archetypal energies. The characters are unconscious energy representations brought to life in dramatic settings. It is easy in this inner-outer space domain to project the imagination, letting it invent, transpose, and complete any scenario wanted. These myths blast human beings from one end of the galaxy to the other. Campbell's ability to explicate myths in such a way as I have been describing advances psychoanalysis from a reductionistic (chained to unconscious stirrings) to an expansionistic (free to be) approach. Like space, unlived myths are cold and threatening. The space for these *Star Wars'* myths is alive with meaning. The planets are virile bodies floating through a galaxy of possibilities. It is because the characters are so like people today that vicariously becoming anyone of them is easy. Knowledge of what lies in the darkness of outer space is exuberantly sought today. Likewise, the unconscious is a dark distant universe that curiosity so much wants to voyage through. Jung, unlike Freud who saw personal biography as all important, recognized the need to include the biography of the human race, in the form of archetypal images. As he knew, it is often the impersonal projections which have the strongest impact on later personal events. It is true that myths have an impersonal aspect to them. By viewing them optimistically as something which is created to foster human wisdom, they become now personally relevant. The personal can aid in uniting an inner with an outer space, as the work of transforming the impersonal into something meaningful and livable is undertaken.

Luke's departure or call to adventure occurs in his young adult years after the death of his uncle, symbolic of Luke's old way of life, leaving him free to follow his destiny. Luke cannot even contain himself to one planet, but must extend himself to all the possibilities the galaxy offers. Luke soon finds his guide and helper, Obi-Wan Kenobe, one who has been through what he is about to face. Thus Luke accepts the opportunity to learn about the Force and how to direct it. He lacks some patience and is a bit overzealous at times, but he is quite willing to endure whatever trials come along. The name "Obi-Wan Kenobe" is itself rather fascinating: O-be-one/Can-no-be; the idea of being and nonbeing, that is, of one who has integrated the opposites in his psyche. The name further suggests fulfilling one's potential or not. It is a matter of choice. Luke, like Obi-Wan, will choose the path of integration. (For a further discussion on the significance of Obi-Wan's name, see page 64 of Waller).

Luke encounters all sorts of strange creatures during the initiation stage of his journey. These creatures represent the many parts of himself that he must recognize and integrate. He actually goes to a world full of mysterious creatures to train as a Jedi Knight with Yoda, the master of masters. He learns to control and direct the Force by quieting his mind. All of his training is in preparation for the intuitive skills he will need at his disposal when he confronts his own dark side. Some of his greatest leaps in consciousness are his struggles which take place within the "forest," a place to confront monsters. Parallel to this is Gilgamesh in the forest fighting Humbaba and the Bull of Heaven. The children in fairy tales, likewise, must travel through the forest and overcome its dark powers, like Hansel and Gretel doing battle with the witch. Luke is dragged under the muck and mire of refuse by a snake-like creature and nearly crushed by the enclosing walls of this container for waste, but survives by his quick thinking; he destroys Imperial fighters and fires the shot that destroys the Death Star. With each encounter of Luke's skills versus the monsters of the evil Empire he grows stronger. He will need this added strength for the final battle will be with the devil himself: Vader.

The return part of Luke's first cycle as a developing hero is that he has helped to save the Rebel Alliance from defeat. And mostly he has gained some mastery over the Force. It is this development which allows Luke to be successful and such a welcomed asset to his people.

The second cycle and second departure to adventure begins when Luke travels to Yoda's world to undergo arduous training to develop his skills as a Jedi Knight to their fullest. He is put through all sorts of tests. Physically, he must develop strong, flexible muscles and endurance. He learns to direct the Force with more accuracy and greater effect by concentration and mental discipline. When Yoda levitates and moves Luke's sinking ship to dry land, Luke learns that the limits to life are within his own mind. Luke's impatience and ambition often interfere with smooth transitions from one stage of his journey to the next, although this is quite common among heroic figures.

Luke's second initiation begins when his friends are captured by Darth Vader and their lives threatened. When Luke learns that his friends are in trouble, he decides against the better judgment of Yoda to come to their rescue. Yoda fears that Luke is too impatient and that his skills are not developed sufficiently to confront an ominous presence such as Vader. Luke believes that he can manage himself well and departs to help his friends. Leia and Chewbacca manage to escape, but Han Solo is put into carbon freeze. Luke is not able to help him because he has been put to the test with Vader and lost a hand. However, he did not succumb to the dark side and refused to join Vader. In the last of these three stories, Luke does rescue Han and defeats the Empire, saving the Alliance.

Luke's second return is different from the first cycle in that Luke is not returning only with victories over objective forces, namely the Empire and Vader, but is bringing back to the world that which is most important, himself. Luke has developed self-knowledge through his ordeals as a Jedi and will need these skills of intuition and insight to train the next Jedi, his sister.

The archetypes abound in these myths and have many roles to play to complete the story about the life of this hero. But his journey is not complete until he slays the biggest monster. This is Vader, who happens to be his father, a former Jedi turned evil. Gordon writes that Vader is a "source of demonic energy," and represents the possibility for evil in Luke (*Empire* 314-15). It is at this meeting that Luke well might be persuaded to identify with the dark side of the Force and go his father's way. Luke has learned from his encounters with Vader that "the Dark Side of the Force can 'consume' him if he is not careful" (Gordon "Power" 202). His father is really the shadow part of himself. Luke fights him but refuses to kill him, because he knows there is good still in him. However, the confrontation between father and son, and the loss of Luke's father's hand, nearly causes his own death (Wyatt 607). The shadow is too powerful to confront casually. Luke cannot destroy his own dark side, but must integrate it. Vader's white "pit" of a head reminds the audience of the tender, quiet person with whom Vader refused to identify and instead became the dark shelled figure (*Ibid*). Luke intuitively knows there is still good remaining in his father and actually turns his father back to identifying with the good side of the Force just before his father relinquishes his spirit and dies. The visual image accompanying this moment is rather poignant because Luke is seen carrying his father "on his shoulders out of the wreckage of the past" (*Ibid* 606). The next time Vader is seen, he is in an ethereal realm with the other Jedi masters. Vader's real name "Annakin Skywalker" gives a hint that he will be reunited to the good side of the Force. Annakin means "and again" I can be one who walks in the sky above the shadow of darkness. Vader did not die, but was transformed into an ally.

The anima is personified in the character of princess Leia. She is introduced to the audience as an arrogant, self-centered woman who expects everyone to bow to her every wish. As Leia observes the unselfish acts of those around her, including the brash Han Solo, who like Leia is out for himself but changes into a courageous unselfish hero in his own right, she, too, begins to change. She moves from an antagonist to Han to being his girlfriend. Her love for Han is evident when she risks her life to save him after he has been given to Jabba the Hut. Her feelings for Luke change from one who is in competition with him (sibling rivalry) to one who intuitively knows Luke is in trouble and demands that the escaping spacecraft return to rescue him. Telepathy in this film is common among people who have close emotional and biological ties, and later it is revealed that Leia is indeed Luke's sister. Yet Luke's anima seems to project less onto any woman and more onto his chthonic environments in which he lives and develops. He is the savior of the Mother archetype much as people are learning today to appreciate their Mother Earth. The strong anima-animus interplay occurs between Leia and Han. They are the princess and knight who are drawn to each other.

This brings up the animus archetype worn by Han and Luke. Han is the spacejock, the flamboyant vagabond who thinks himself to be a lady's man, thus his self-assuredness that Leia is very fond of him, which at first Leia denies, because she is too involved with herself and her own projection of meeting the perfect "macho" man. When Han and Leia's projections begin to lack intensity and the two of them incorporate psychological material into their psyches, they see each other for who each is and just happen to like what they see. Luke, too, is a macho type figure who is even referred to as a knight. What more could any princess want? Except in this case the true knight is her brother, thus a projection onto him could not work. Han is the next likely and suitable candidate for Leia's unconscious to seek out.

The self archetype is the most powerful force in Luke's life. And the self is personified in the characters of Obi-Wan and Yoda, the two most integrated personalities in the tale. They are Luke's guiding light, his conscience, source of inspiration and example of what can be done. In fact, to borrow from von Franz, they act as the *daimon* or "inner guru" who show Luke the way (150). It is not a coincidence that Yoda lives on a swamp planet that is primitive in appearance. Yoda is an integrated mother-father archetype and a transpersonal entity who, to use Neumann's words, speaks the collective voice that changes worlds (*Origins* 174). His home is the archaic realm from which the archetypes emerge and the place of Luke's most necessary training. It is the center out of which Luke emerges a more integrated personality. The name "Yoda" appears to be a derivative of the sanskrit word "yuddha" standing for battle. Yoda is the being that must instruct Luke how to battle the dark side of his soul, as well as how it is personified in the person of Darth Vader. Yoda is the father of the Jedis, and the one who gathers his disciples' unguided energies together and unites them for creative interaction with the Force.

Chapter Eight

The Feminine Presence in Myths: An Ethical Imperative

I have discussed the heroic quest in the *Star Wars'* myths. This quest revealed a world dominated and imagined by males. *Star Wars* does not stand alone. For each myth that I have detailed reveals this male dominated *weltanschauung* (worldview). The protagonists in every case were men, such that the adventures were about men, primarily. These adventures bared a world created by a dominating masculine consciousness. Where are the females in these tales? They are there, and yet, their roles are shadowy by comparison to those of the males. What is most interesting is that the males in these tales could not have survived or have been nearly as successful without the females.

Gilgamesh has his Siddhuri, who advises him to enjoy the fruits of life, for it is not meant for human beings to live forever. She is his practical advisor. Even though Gilgamesh rejects her proposal, in the end, this is very much what he does. She knows the inevitable, Gilgamesh has not learnt this lesson, yet. Being a king does not free him from the ultimate human challenges. Utnapishtim's wife is another important woman (and she is not even given a name). It is she who reveals the location of the restorative plant to Gilgamesh. The fact that he fails in using it is not her fault. Her motherly instinct does its best to watch over him. But boys cannot be protected by their mothers forever.

Arjuna's nurturing counselor is the feminine principle embodied in Krishna. Krishna is the incarnation of the World Soul guiding Arjuna to unite the battling urges within himself. It is Krishna who reveals to Arjuna the mysteries of Ultimate

Reality. Without the Krishna force Arjuna would be just another warrior.

Owein has his lady Lunet who frees him from certain death by moving him to safety in her chamber. In addition, she arranges a marriage between him and her Lady.

Luke has his sister Leia who psychically knows he is alive on Cloud City and returns for him. Should it seem odd that the strongest feminine presences come from Obi-Wan and Yoda? They are the most realized, having integrated their yin and yang, anima and animus. It is their guiding, nurturing, consoling natures which Luke, later on, must absorb into himself. These two guardian spirits have transcended the male-female polarity. Yet, it is their gentle, non-forceful (feminine) side that they present to Luke. As this is the part of himself that is still needing to be more fully realized.

It is the female consciousness, the feminine principle that is in the background to these myths. Whether they find embodiment in a physical woman or female being is not of primary importance to make the story work. Although, it is significant. Why are not Luke's spiritual teachers females? The task then becomes a search for the heroine. The real question being—is the hero's journey only for males? And if it is not, then why are not the myths full of heroines? The rest of my discussion shall lead us to answering these questions, and the implications they pose. And suggestions for furthering the feminine presence in myths and in life.

It becomes apparent that these heroes could not have succeeded without the female presence. In each case it is a woman whose contribution made the story a success. The macho animus without the knowing anima would have followed an empty destiny. The boyish, undirected passion of these men is given direction by the feminine personas.

The spectacle of the twentieth century has seen momentous changes in the roles of and attitudes toward women. There is still much to do in the way of social and attitudinal changes by those suppressing women. In order to understand better how these attitudes arose, perhaps it will be useful to look at the role of men and women in the early planting and hunting societies. I shall claim that a fear of women developed and contributed to misogynous attitudes. I should like to discuss how men came to subvert women.

The earliest archeological evidence of worship is in the form of female goddess statues placed on shrines (paleolithic sites), and the emphasis being on their genitals and breasts (Campbell *Primitive* 313). The female body was viewed as life-affirming, generative, and prolific. She was identified with "mother" earth, as it is the body in which plants grow and from which animals drink. Men and women alike worshipped the mother goddess.

During the late paleolithic period, hunting peoples diminished the importance of the goddess. The hunting groups increased in numbers, traveled warmer regions, and tracked herds of animals. Women's domestic activities dwindled in importance to the men's hunting skills. A masculine psychology developed "with an emphasis on achievement—and women became ancillaries to male achievement" (Downing 99-100).

Women in planting societies made the earth appear to come alive, as they made their transition from gatherers to cultivators of the land. Thus, they "enjoyed a magico-religious and social advantage" (Downing 100). Agricultural society became favorable to men with the advent of the plow. It required physical strength, and once again the women's roles were overshadowed. Social stratification took on new meaning, as men became the leaders, and imposed their rule by force (*Ibid*). In fact, Joseph Campbell wrote that the magic and awe of the female, experienced by the earliest humans, was a wonder of the universe. "This gave to women a prodigious power," which men have sought to "break, control, and employ to their own ends" (*Primitive* 315).

The forceful and violent response by men towards women most likely developed over a lengthy period. Initially, men found themselves doing socially perceived inferior tasks. The men must have grown resentful of women. They tried to sublimate their hostile feelings through rituals signifying the leaving behind of the mother. Their "men's clubs" gave them standing in their newly formed society. Men's roles, in fact, became socially significant. The men developed a sense of self-worth, and reinforced this by refusing the women exploration of their own potentials. Men had developed a psychological fear of the feminine. Men allowed images of masculine futility to drift into their collective unconscious, where, unchecked by reason, a fear of the female goddess arose. In Jungian terms, these men feared recognition, acceptance, and integration of the anima with their animus. Archetypes are polar in nature, and therefore union is demanded. The goddess within emerged in the very rituals in which the men attempted to deny her access. The men crawled through the uterine passage into the cave's womb from which their rituals came to birth. Fear of the feminine became repressed in the male psyche; subservient roles were imposed on women. In time, this subordination of the female became part of the social structure.

Repressed in these male psyches and what became misdirected at women in general was a fear of the Great Mother. She is bisexual, containing within her yin and yang. She is *wu chi*, undifferentiated void from which life erupts. The yang or masculine consciousness no longer regarded the Great Mother as the one who nourishes, protects, and comforts. As the yang element gained its independence, the Mother became the terrifying devourer of all who wished their freedom. She was now pointed to as the force which stood in the way of developing consciousness and human progress (Colegrave 42-43). Of course, even this nature becomes polarized in the goddess figures. Ishtar is Gilgamesh's gentle seductress or when rejected becomes his worst nightmare. The Hindu goddess Kali is one moment associated with creation and fertility, the next with death and decay. Hence, as it is the Mother that is believed to impede human development, the generalization onto all women occurs. Now women, specifically, become the typification of evil.

A distinction needs to be drawn between the bisexual Great Mother archetype and the anima, feminine principled archetype. The struggle is against the Mother not the feminine. Actually, the feminine, too, is as much a result of the masculine struggle for independence. The power needed to make this break was so great that a change of consciousness occurred leaving the memories of this struggle far behind. The masculine psyche forgot and repressed the painful separation, and in so doing, associated the feminine part of the psyche with the Mother. This misrepresentation led to the dragon woman syndrome, feeling that women would devour their manly usefulness. Until men remove this fear from their psyches, women will continue to be victimized. The Eden myth when viewed free of repression, recognizes that it was the powerful feeling nature of Eve which moved Adam, not to fall from paradise, but to leap into self-consciousness. Human beings took the first step from remaining instinctually driven animals to being self-conscious co-creators of their destinies. They were no longer pilotless ships cast about on a tempestuous sea, ignorant of the journey being made upon them. They now became captains with the ability to chart a course straight to their own unique destiny. In order to plot life's course accurately, people must recognize the various patterns which take shape in their lives. Failure to actively engage with life's changing patterns can result in life living each person, rather than each person living life.

These myths which I have written about are personified in a male's world, that is, they reflect a male point of view. They are written to entertain men; to show off manly virtues; to exhibit man as warrior. These "guys" are always fighting. Gilgamesh cannot get enough roughnecking. Owein goes out of his way to test his combat skills. Luke lives in a world that is continuously at war. And Arjuna wonders whether he should slay his kinfolk. No one wants to sit down at the "roundtable" and talk. Except Arjuna, who engages in dialogue with Krishna, but even this is a very philosophical conversation. His feelings, which are the original reason for him questioning his duty, are now pushed back so that he can analyze the situation. His conclusion is to do his duty and fight. What happened to his feelings? Though some realization of the anima occurred, a good portion of it fell back into the unconscious. Luke learns at each crucial moment of his journey that it is his feelings which guide him to victory and save his life. Gilgamesh's whole journey is motivated by his feelings to make a name for himself; and after grieving over the death of Enkidu, to achieve immortality.

Surprisingly, though he lived at a time when empiricism and rationalism dominated the intellectual community, Freud courageously welcomed the insights gained by exploring the feeling-tone of the unconscious. Jung was pleased to have as a teacher one who was able and ready to venture into the emotions and open a new world of inquiry. Freud's free association test, and Jung's later word association test, are sound scientific tools for probing unconsciously generated feelings. Myths contain a wealth of feeling-tone images to be scrutinized and connected with personal experiences. If after free associating, people do not discover anything meaningful or significant, then they can move on to another image. Beyond this, creatively imagining what it would be like to be a Luke, Leia, or a Wookie can be insightful and cathartic in itself. Creative fantasizing may be what is needed to move into a more fruitful mode of activity. Insights gained from such exploration can be applied to daily tasks which can become more alive because they are being participated in with greater consciousness.

It appears that the most able heroes are those who can find a balance between their rational and irrational natures. It is the emotions which motivate and inspire. Feelings are the bodily sensations of these forces and drives. Thoughts and intellect are then used to interpret, organize, and direct these forces. Luke shows that the best direction comes from the release of conscious control. The intuitive mind transcends the rational mind. The rational mind can make mistakes. It separates and divides. The intuitive mind answers to the whole. It integrates and heals. Those who are led strictly by their feelings tend to discriminate poorly, which can lead to many errors in judgment. They respond to what is most stimulating to the senses and, in so doing, often neglect the longer-term consequences of their actions. Those who think their way through situations, believing themselves to be quite logical, often undervalue what is most important. Their lack of feelings causes them to be cold and calculating. Empathy is often lacking in their response to others. It is a matter of

The Feminine Presence in Myths

uniting feeling and thinking, cooperation and competition, the undifferentiated with the differentiated. Persons who reason on their feelings to understand them more clearly, while simultaneously remembering to answer to their heart seem to be the most well-adjusted. An ongoing dialogue between the emotive and cognitive faculties is necessary to maintain a harmonic resonating of psychic energies. If either faculty is continuously dominating, then polarization with its lopsidedness ensues.

Arjuna used his reason to arrive at his answers. However, with the appearance of the god Krishna, Arjuna's higher nature, he receives insights into the very fabric of mindstuff. He has intuitive leaps of understanding. These moments transcend feeling or thinking. He is no longer originating and creating his reality, but responding to the fullness of his nature. Likewise, does Luke do, when he lets the Force flow through him. This sort of transcendental intuition lets them be conscious without being in the "I am" consciousness. They are not thinking or responding in terms of polarity, but have now transcended this dualistic mode of being. Their psychology is now transpersonal.

I feel that the feminine saturates these mythological worlds much like the clouds in a Taoist landscape painting drift over mountains, while their translucent arms stroke the gently rolling fields, settling on the valleys far below. The Western mind tends to analyze the Taoist painting or mythic tales dissecting them into minute parts. It focuses on the most colorful and unusual. It may fail to realize the gestalt or whole. The Taoist blends the parts together into one story. It is the feminine in myths which connect all the disparate parts together. Even the Force is feminine. It is responsive, accepting, and non-judgmental. It does not question whether it is a Darth Vader or a Luke Skywalker who wishes to use It, It simply gives. It is energy, ever-ready and always available. Only self-conscious beings choose how to use It, and pass judgment on whether the use of It is good or evil, right or wrong. Animals respond to It instinctively, never asking It for anything nor cursing It when they do not get what they need.

As I have been examining the masculine and feminine principles of the psyche, I have been wondering what attributes the female heroine must express. The Western mind associates compassion, gentleness, and kindness with the feminine. Most models of the heroine are compassionate, life-affirming, nurturing, and consoling. They must, like heroes, depart from the accepted way of doing things. They will battle bureaucracy; encounter prejudice and discrimination; be physically and emotionally abused because they are physically less strong than their male counterparts. Mythically, these champions escape from the confines of a domineering master, husband, or father. They know there is a better way to live than the submissive role these oppressive figures encourage in them. Or even if these grand females are well-provided for, they recognize that the environment in which they live must be expanded to include the murmurings of the heart. Heroines wander off into the forest, encountering giants, dark magicians, and other ominous creatures. They have helpers along the way, as do all who make the journey into inner space. And they return with an elixir of life; as helping servants; or as healers. The unsettling aspect of viewing heroines as gentle is that some perceive this as a weakness. They still believe that these women are in need of being rescued by the strong male. Women who are truly heroic, knowing how to work with their yin and yang energies, are certainly as capable as any men.

Heroines are warriors too, and once in a while they must pickup a sword. Most often, they slay demons with their hearts. Heroes tend to do battle with the thoughts; heroines with the feelings. Heroes anatomize everything and divide their spoils. Heroines return everything to its proper place and unite. Both become more complete because of this process, only they accomplish this differently. The next stage for the heroes is to incorporate more compassion into their psyches. The heroines next step is to learn to put on a little body armor when called to do so. This does not mean that they have to become violent, just be able to protect themselves from the gross injustices of the world. And the men, already able-bodied, need to open themselves to the nurturing, empathic forces in the universe.

If I were to cease my comments on the quests of the heroes and heroines, now, then I might leave the readers with a one-sided and distorted impression of these transpirations. Heroines do not necessarily have to be first compassionate, anima driven women to be recognized as successful questors. They might be muscle building, animus potent gladiators, inspired by an inner vision to rid the world of corruption and vice. The 1991 movie *Terminator II* plays witness to such a woman. She makes a radical change from the naive, bewildered single girl of the first movie, to the alert, confident mother of the second film. She is not only the protector of her own son, but of the entire human race. She dresses in battle fatigues, has well-developed muscles, and can easily outsmart and subdue a handful of men. The gentle side of her nature is well submerged in the duties of her present role.

I want to make it clear that whether people are heroes or heroines, and whether they start off their journey as anima or animus baring individuals, their adventure is not finished. To make the transition from attachment to the "mother" to becoming an independent individual, the animus must dominate. The animus is what separates individual consciousness from the psychoid mind of a child. This is the mythological leaving of the garden of paradise. The Adam and Eve who before eating from the tree of knowledge had no awareness of their nakedness. They had no concept of "other." They interacted with each other as do animals, in a state of simple-consciousness. Self-consciousness had not yet arisen. This was a later development in human evolution. Colegrave iterates this point writing that the Great Mother reigned over a "pre-polarized consciousness, a stage of psychological development when everything appeared to be embraced in one undifferentiated unity. The masculine consciousness had not yet split human awareness into subject and object" (xi). The separating quality of the animus was needed to make this leap in consciousness. Just as all children must leave the care and protection of their mothers, the human race had to leave the blissful ignorance of a life spent with the Great Mother. This was and is part of the evolution of consciousness. Myths mirror these transitional stages of human consciousness. The Great Mother myths begin the journey of human beings, revealing a world held together by the great arms of the Mother Goddess. Next, come the myths of the warriors, having awaken in the powerful masculine psyche. They reveal a consciousness which seeks to recognize the many manifestations of life. The Mother has not disappeared, but has simply begun to count her children. And the children now know of their many brothers and sisters. After making the break with the consciousness of the undifferentiated void, and becoming self-responding individuals, a return must be made. This return is not to a void empty of form, but to one which is now given form by free and self-aware individuals. The movement in consciousness is from a state of undifferentiated not knowing; to differentiated knowing; to undifferentiated knowing, with the ability for differentiating as needed. Colegrave elucidates this point so well when she writes:

> The birth of a masculine and feminine way of seeing the world does not deny the insights of the matriarchal consciousness but, by expanding, deepening, and clarifying them, prepares for a later stage of development in which both principles can meet in a psychological marriage leading individuals back to the harmony of the Great Mother and knowing it consciously and freely for the first time (49).

The myths of the twentieth century have peaked in their animus statement of identity and individuality. They have also revealed the wounds and scars of such a one-sided brother, father, son dominated worldview. The earlier Great Mother and goddess myths could not stand alone, indefinitely. Each of these transitional periods left their scars. The myths of the future, and this future is now, must present a world in which the anima and animus find compatible expression. Campbell wrote that myths are not predictable, but I believe that they can be sensed. Myths are tales which reveal the inner paths of societies. They also respond to the group consciousness at the time they are written. And within these groups, there is always one or more who is ahead of these times, and who exceeds and surpasses the groups in which they live. Within these individuals own consciousnesses will be found the next stage for the future group myth. The personal mythic-mystical stories of these few pioneers will show the way to the future. And if there are those who are very adept at recognizing the patterns and trends of a society, then they can know to near certainty the next step to be taken.

The next stage is transpersonal, transcendental, mystical, the Tao beyond the yin and yang. The new myths must be about those who have united the anima with animus, or put another way, have synthesized the psyche's masculine and feminine principles. It is more than the recognition that positive and negative are relative conditions and that their potential differences establish the direction that they will take (Taimni 74). They will move from being dipolar to monopolar. Afterall, polarities by their very nature imply unity, regardless of whether differences can be extracted from them. This is a movement towards becoming androgynous in nature. The portrayal of such individuals in myths will be of sage-like beings. They are the Obi-Wans and Yodas. These are the persons who have made the transformation of consciousness, from that of self- to cosmic-consciousness. And yet, it is more than achieving the awareness associated with these higher states, also referred to as *nirvana, moksha,* Christ consciousness, or *satori*. The awareness alone is not sufficient for ongoing inner peace and the global sense of responsibleness and life-affirming attitude that is conditioned by these experiences. Awareness or enlightenment is only the first giant step towards the release of consoling energies. Those who experience higher consciousness must learn through steely discipline to apply these new insights to their daily living. These revelations gained during peak moments of consciousness can only continue to remain vibrantly affective when practiced diligently. It is through the continued experiences of life, reasoning upon those experiences, and allowing the feelings of those events to penetrate the self, that will cause the disciples of the quest to continue to grow and develop in consciousness.

Transforming consciousness is similar to athletic development. Athletes must continually ingest what they have learned from their workouts and apply it to their next practices.

Doing the movements without an image to stabilize them, might produce bodies that are well-conditioned, but not ones that express proficiency. Actions need to be inwardly guided. Going through the actions does not make people good athletes any more than reading books makes them good thinkers. This is why people who use drugs to induce an altered state of consciousness are unable to maintain such a condition. They may, momentarily, be able to experience a unified reality, but that in itself is far from being enlightened. Once the effect of the chemical diminishes, they will return to their usual perceptual state. Jesus spoke of this when he said that there will always be those, who like thieves, will try to enter heaven through the back door. Enlightenment is more than a glimpse at a unified cosmos or an undifferentiated whole. It is human beings understanding how to live a moral existence, while simultaneously continuing to develop their selfhood in relationship to the world community. It is not impressive to exhibit inner peace while living in a mountaintop cave isolated from others. The true sage is able to come down from the mountain, live amongst the chaos, and continue radiating an aura of calm.

I believe that the concept of "androgyny" is useful in understanding the transforming of consciousness. It comes from the Greek "andro" (male) and "gyne" (female). It was Aristophanes who used it when referring to the lost half of a person. Thus love became the seeking after the lost portion of oneself. The male sought for the female and the female looked to unite with the male. Plato suggested through Aristophanes that the human being was originally both male and female in physical appearance. These beings were split in two as punishment for transgressing against the gods. Love became the search for one's other half (Weber 73). Psychologically speaking, it is not true that humans are only male or only female, and that physically uniting with one of the other sex will somehow make them whole. Human beings are whole, right now, psychically both male and female. What they are not, is complete. The way in which I am using androgyny is not the search for wholeness, but completion. The anima and animus, yin and yang are in all persons already. Consequently everyone is whole, that is, all the psychical elements that each person needs is in them already. The journey then becomes the search for putting these elements together in the proper pattern and relationship, that permits the harmonious interchange of energy between and within every part of a person. An assembly line consists of many parts waiting to be put together. Each part is perfect as it exists by itself. And when seen as being a part of the overall image is recognized as being whole. Everything is there that is supposed to be there. Nothing else is needed but to bring these elements together into a functioning unit and thus make the image complete. The assembly line parts for a car are perfect and whole, but not yet complete until they are united properly. Most human beings are not complete because their various bodily systems are not working in cooperation with each other. An automobile cannot function completely unless each part is in the right relationship with every other part. A man who falls in love with a particular woman is making a marriage with the temporal. This relationship is fine and often necessary, but he must realize that the marriage that will remain with him long after his human wife has ceased to exist, is the union with his own eternal feminine. Finding completion in another person is an illusion, and an obstacle to real union. Union with another person should be treated as a complete relationship within itself. Not as a substitution for completing the journey within oneself.

The educational systems, for the most part, have not been responsive in transforming consciousness. They tend to be dedicated to conveying information and informing people "what" to think. Students learn that memorizing data is what will lead to a high grade for the course. Students, children, and all people who are being educated need to be taught in a manner promoting self-growth through the continued reasoning on experiences. And even this is not adequate if what is encouraged is to be a thinking, analyzing, comparing sort of person. The feeling side must also be attended to. Gathering information equals knowledge, having experiences and reasoning on them, making comparisons, analyzing the data equals understanding, and being aware of the sorts of feelings which unleash the vital forces of life and how to direct them can lead to wisdom. Socrates said that the word "educate" means to draw out of one what is already within. It is not putting stuff into the pupils. The Taoists were concerned with this attitude as well. Lao Tzu, the Chinese philosopher spoke of the "uncarved block." This is like the condition of a young child, untouched by the molding ambitions of society. The very young are the unsculpted clay, the undyed silk, still yet uncontaminated by other people's ideas. How often do people say to their children after taking them to the zoo; "How did you *like* the zoo?" Why not ask them, "What was your experience of the zoo" or "How did you feel about going to see the animals" or "What did you think about the trip to the zoo today?" Persons tend to present the desired answers by the way they pose the questions.

The "ethical imperative" in which I subtitled this chapter is the recognition, acceptance, and integration of the feminine principle with the masculine principle. The twentieth century world is much the result of looking at the world through yang tinted glasses. Yin must also become part of this tint, making the viewing done through androgynous' eyes. The classroom environment needs to be not only the schoolroom, but the world-at-large. Educating people through ways which encourages them "how" to think, and explore their environment, develops self-confidence and self-esteem. Children who are unable to explore their own abilities become the followers of other people's destinies. They do not know what they are capable of doing and becoming. What they do know has been taught to them by others. If they are to awaken their slumbering potentials, and feel the embrace of their own life-affirming energies, then they must develop in an environment which is conducive for self-understanding. This "learning field" will support both anima and animus energies, encouraging the experiencing of each.

Conclusion

I have been investigating how the study of myth provides an integral key to understanding the individual, society, and the world. I hope to have demonstrated that through myths human beings integrate better the diverse dimensions of their experiences into a workable life-system. The study of myth is, therefore, a responsible way to understand both psychological and socio-cultural influences on human beings.

Any mythopoeic literature provides a channel through which people can meet and explore the varied interests and experiences of other peoples. Myths provide potential insights into the culture, religion, and the history of those other peoples. They bring together the thoughts of the ancients with those of modern-day thinkers, revealing their similarities and differences. By looking in retrospect at the foundational patterns undergirding history, individuals are better able to discern what is relevant and valuable for people today. Mythology enables moderns to make connections with the past and, with the information gained, to resolve contemporary dilemmas.

Myths provide participants with the development of a personalized value system. Such a system would consider people's responses for coping and relating to each other and to life. Recent archeological discoveries have been able to piece together lost documents about myths, such as ancient texts from the Near East, as well as to compile tales from oral traditions where the myth is still "living and functioning in society" (Knox 118). Myths today, even of other cultures, affect the readers because of the archetypal power within them. Information about the content of myths is continuously being renewed. It is up to people to renew as well an understanding of the value systems inherent in myths.

Studying the world's mythologies can lead to formation of value systems because, beneath all their diversity, myths speak of universal human categories. The content of myths, like that of symbols, is meant to be transcended in that it points to something beyond itself. For example, Hektor and Achilleus in the *Iliad* are symbols of the hero archetype who passed a series of initiation rites, thus answering questions within themselves about life. Odysseus of the *Odyssey* personifies the trickster archetype, and the tale itself reveals the journey motif. *Oedipus Rex* still mesmerizes its readers today because of the psychological insights it provides regarding human beings. The depth psychology of its characters is the same as those living today. Campbell wrote: "As the imagery of a dream is metaphorical of the psychology of its dreamer, that of a mythology is metaphorical of the psychological posture of the people to whom it pertains" (*Inner Reaches* 12). People living today may not be Jedi knights and princesses, but they are presidents and corporate executives; honor, money, power, manipulation, crisis, decisions, and kindness were, are, and will be part of the human community for a long time. Ancient mythic themes continuously appear in literature: Virgil, Dante, Milton, and Joyce all utilized mythological figures in their writings. Renaissance artists combined classical myths with Christian values. Botticelli incorporated characters such as Venus, Mercury, Cupid, and the Winds of Spring into some of his paintings. And his and all other people's uses invariably carry a deeper meaning for the receiver than the surface connotation. Artists of all sorts have found inspiration from mythological tales. References to myths continue to be found in everyday experiences whether people are aware of it or not: Cupid appears on Valentine's Day cards; the winged messenger Mercury is the symbol of some delivery services; a police car has a siren; people might "listen to a kindly mentor or despite a hectoring bully" (Asimov 11). Before someone is about to engage in a challenging activity, one often says today, "May the Force be with you." Thus, "by understanding the myths, people will understand themselves better" (Asimov 12).

It has been my intention throughout this thesis to clarify the concepts regarding Jung's model of the psyche and the personification and function of the archetypes drawn from the various myths. And to explicate how Jung has expanded on Freud's psychoanalytic theories. The psyche may be conceived of as having many layers, the "deeper" ones being less individual and more collective in their nature "until they are universalized and extinguished in the body's materiality" (Jung *Essays on Mythology* 92). In other words, the archetypes are translators of the processes of the biochemical and physiological systems. They interpret how people are grounded to the world. Feinstein asserts that "myths are coded in biochemistry and influenced by biochemical changes" (*Magical Blend* 40). Campbell said in *The Hero's Journey* that "every organ of the body has its energy impulse, and the experience of the conflicts of these different energies inside, is what constitutes the psyche. It's nature talking" (159).

Jung recognized that the unconscious was not something subordinate to Freud's pleasure principle or an isolated unit of the person. It was subject to the organizing principle of the total personality (Frey-Rohn 59). The unconscious has to be organized to provide further clarity to its releasing psychic energies which provide the symbols with which consciousness will interact. Not only are emotional residues of the ancestors stored in the collective unconscious. Freud believed that the unconscious and its affects could be determined and measured. Whereas Jung was more interested in integrating the various affects with the whole of personality. It is most useful to look at myths in light of their parts to the whole. Mythic characters gain their meaning from their relationships to each other. As in dreams, the characters are but the many personalities of the dreamer. Each character represents a different function of the psyche.

Another important inference by Jung is that this multiple psyche logically implies that unity must be its opposite. He realized that the "tension between the tendency to dissociate and the inclination towards unity was a phenomenon intrinsically characteristic of the life process" (Frey-Rohn 69). The nodal point of Jung's psychology is the resolution of conflicting opposites. Jung realized that finding a way to resolve the tension between the opposites led to a renewal of psychic energy, and revealed new, as yet uncharted stratas of the collective unconscious. Probing these new stratas makes possible individuation. It is the reshaping of concepts with their associated behavioral changes that lead to new life patterns being formed. By patterns, I mean the repeated way people respond to various situations. By changing the concepts, new and hopefully better patterns emerge making the interaction with life more pleasant.

Recognizing and integrating the archetypes are part of the process of psychic transformation. The shadow appears in literature as the evil side of life, as monsters and demonic forces. The shadow can be masculine or feminine, or sexless. It is the part of life that destroys without forethought or concern for the wellbeing of others. It is the witch in *Hansel and Gretel*. It is the entity or force that heroic beings must triumph over in order to move on to the next stage of adventure. The shadow, like all the archetypes, is within the heroic figures and is projected outward so that they can confront it. The real confrontation eventually is done within and the projection then ceases or becomes an ally. Robert Bly writes that "every part of the personality that people do not love will become hostile towards them" (13). The anima is the female figure and the animus the male figure in myths. There are instances when a woman strongly identifies with her animus, though a female does not represent the anima figure in the tale. The virgin goddess Artemis denies her femininity and instead develops the skills commonly associated with a man. Men who have an undeveloped animus would be effeminate in their nature as is the god Dionysus. The self is the mandala archetype, the archetype of integration drawing the other archetypes together toward completeness. It is personified in such figures as the wise old man, the oriental sage and the female prophetess.

These transformations of consciousness for twentieth-century human beings will be scarce until people become aware that myths are constructed of patterns which when recognized can lead to an understanding of what human beings are and how they fit into the schema of life. Myths are more than stories about gods; they are the umbilical cord to God, linking the collective and individual destinies to the very fabric of life itself—the center from which the power of being radiates. They nourish the imagination which is the heart of the soul. Myths satisfy the most primal and spiritual appetites, supplying persons with the needed strength to fulfill the heroic adventure. Until people fully live the mythic image, they cannot afford to have the cord cut.

I hope to have demonstrated in this thesis that myths are the emergence of unconscious patterns from the psyche into the field of conscious participation. Campbell wrote that one must approach the world without preconceptions, evaluating and creating, not simply imitating "inherited patterns of thought and action, but becoming an innovating center, an active, creative center of the life process" (*Myths to Live By* 47). Myths represent the collective patterns or archetypes of society (Sanford 6) with an emphasis on the potential for individuation within each person (Jung *Man & Symbols* 169-70). The internalization of symbols as part of a personal journey is thus the power behind myths. Myths make statements about the fundamental patterns of life's conditions, and thereby they shape and direct communal and individual destinies. They teach the feeling of being alive. They deal with inner values by harmonizing the goal-oriented outer values with subjective experiences. Life is energy in billions of patterns (Watts 13), eating, reproducing, and dying in endlessly repeating cycles. The meaning of this exchange of energy is what people make it. Meaning is not inherent in the universe as those who are self-conscious are the masters of their own destinies. Human beings are energy that has become self-aware, self-conscious, and hence co-creators with "That Which Is," the unnameable that is beyond all conceptualizations. Myths are a way of freeing this energy so that people can guide and direct it. Myths thus bring people into a level of consciousness that is spiritual while simultaneously liberating them from cultural chains.

Once again, a psychoanalytic interpretation of personal events is not satisfactory for working with the whole person. Jung supplies a non-reductive theory where impersonal, archetypal, mythic images can be empowered. As Jung pointed out a "reductive procedure breaks down at the point where the dream symbols can no longer be reduced to personal reminiscences, that is, when the images of the collective unconscious begin to appear" (*CW* 7:80-81). Jung's emphasis on the archetypal, in addition to the personal experiences, suggests myths to be cross-cultural and timeless. Newer symbols may replace older ones, but their themes remain constant.

It is fairly obvious to discern the symbols in make-believe stories where the characters and events are consciously invented to portray particular emotion-filled experiences. For example, television will portray an old man begging in front of the capital building, to show the disregard politicians have for human welfare. People's own lives are much more complex and full of "behind the scene" episodes that would lack entertainment value as make-believe stories. Neumann wrote that myths are "always the unconscious representation of such crucial life situations" (*Amor & Psyche* 65). Myths represent the ideals in human beings. Tales are not heard wherein the protagonist discusses with her mother the best brand of laundry detergent to use. Myths do not trivialize human affairs, rather they make manifest those elements which need to be incorporated into life. Symbols of power are needed to move people from dormancy to activity. People must remain conscious that "the myth" lies within. It is more than a make-believe story; it is a way of life, a chance, an opportunity, an experience to be had. The mythic elements in life shout from their unconscious origins. They offer a window to the soul through the unconscious. Personal mythic journeys need not be a battle with dragons, evil rulers, the rescue of a princess, or to travel to remote planets. These are all symbols in myths of the journey and awakening of the self within the Self.

Luke's overcoming his self-doubt to remain with Yoda and continue to train or to rescue his friends is likewise anyone's moment of choice. All persons decide whom to wed, what career to pursue, where to live, where to work, whether to be parents, and so on. Perhaps each of these appear less glamorous than the adventures of mythic heroes and heroines; yet, they are as necessary to the quest, in the search, for a valuable and meaningful existence.

I hope that I have demonstrated in the analysis of the four myths the universal appearance of the archetypes and the repeatable stages to the heroic journey. I should encourage the recognition and desire by people to locate these archetypes within their lives, so that integration of them will occur more readily. In addition, it will be most useful for all to locate the heroes or heroines within themselves. Using the three Campbellian stages of the heroic journey will inform the participants as to where they need to go. Unconscious energies have been actualized in myths from distant locales and distinct ages, thus revealing the universality of their symbols and metaphors. More important is that these myths are a reminder of the possibilities for self-discovery and participation. They render it possible to discriminate that which is useful from that which leads people astray from the experiences of life. Myths literally are within. Persons can refuse to live the myths and let them live them. Or people can plunge into the very fabric of life itself, being a co-creating force of destiny. How many have died leaving nothing more than the dash on their tombstone between their date-of-birth and death as their experience of living? People who live a mythless existence live an empty life. Myths must be created that are culturally acceptable and personally meaningful, utilizing the symbols of today which are yet alive.

There appear to be two currents along which modern day myths are traveling. One is the development of a "personal mythology." Jung refers to this idea in his autobiography by telling his "personal myth" (*Memories* 3). This involves a journey back into the personal unconscious, in addition to entering the collective unconscious. What must be travelled is the Thesean labyrinth into the dark cave wherein dwells the psychic monster. But more must be done than confront this monster only, for all carry a two-edged sword, and in the slaying of it, will wound themselves. There is absolutely no possibility of ever escaping or avoiding the personification of innerpsychic forces. The best that can be done is to acknowledge their existence, learn how they function, temporarily adapt to those forces which seem beyond one's control, and learn to direct their energies into constructive channels of expression. To deny them is like placing a hand over the hole in the dam to stop the pressure of the water. In a short while, the pressure will blow out the hole countless of times larger than if the water had been rechanneled at the first indication that something was wrong.

A personal mythology will draw the participants into itself to discern the emotional patterns that generate behavior (Feinstein *Common Boundary* 18). This process requires a degree of discipline and mastery over conscious desires, and hence, doing not one's will, but the will of the "Mother-Father" within—namely, the archetypal unconscious. Furthermore, a personal mythology in order to be affective must remind people of their relationship with the outside world and how to be in rapport with it. If they are unable to adapt to the environment, then a personal mythology will only be useful if lived in isolation which is impossible as nothing exists apart from anything else. Myth's purpose is to transform people from the center of their being outward. People learn to be in this world while not being of it. For the world all are truly a part of is that of the psyche and its transpersonal and spiritual processes.

The other aspect of myths is the need for a "world mythology." Feinstein states that humankind is in need of a mythology which "allows more diversity and promotes greater cooperation. People are being required to create a worldwide mythology" (*Magical Blend* 39). What is lacking are twentieth century symbols that would unify people's alleged differences. The world's major religions point to the same place, but as their symbols are culturally tainted, people unwittingly identify with the outward appearance, rather than with the transcendental reality behind the symbols. Hoeller writes that a person whose psyche is highly individuated, and thus is a very conscious being, participates in eternity. Psychic wholeness is everlasting and imperishable (26). Living a myth fully in life will more assuredly render the likelihood of a world mythology. I mean by this that people must recognize the undergirding patterns to Ultimate Reality. They first do this by recognizing the patterns of their own experiences. Learning to work with these psychical energies and forces that permeate being will develop into a healthy-minded philosophy. The world is full of transitory differences and objects fleeting into and out of existence. It is the unifying themes that garnish life and are with what is to be identified. In a very real way future mythologies must incorporate the mystical unifying principle into their very core in order for people to vicariously or directly participate in the psychic healing that they offer. This is what I mean by world mythology: not another religion or separating philosophy, nor something that operates from technique or fad. It must consist of the universal laws saturating all life, holding it together, and unifying its many ways of expressing.

Bibliography

Abusch, T. "Ishtar's Proposal and Gilgamesh's Refusal: An Interpretation of the Gilgamesh Epic, Tablet 6, Lines 1-679". *History of Religions.* 26.2 (Nov. 1986): 143-187.

Asimov, I. *Words from the Myths.* 1961. New York: Signet, 1969.

Aurobindo, S. *Essays on the Gita.* New York: Sri Aurobindo Library, 1950.

Beane, W. C., and W. G. Doty, eds. *Myths, Rites, and Symbols: A Mircea Eliade Reader.* New York: Harper & Row, 1976.

Bettelheim, B. *The Uses of Enchantment: The Meaning and Importance of Fairy Tales.* 1975. New York: Vintage, 1977.

Beye, C. R. "Gilgamesh, Lolita, and Huckleberry Finn." *Classical and Modern Literature,* 9.1 (Fall 1988): 39-50.

Bidney, D. "Myth, Symbolism, and Truth." *Myth: A Symposium.* Ed. T. A. Sebeok. Philadelphia: American Folklore Society, 1955.

Bly, R. "The Long Bag We Drag Behind Us." *Magical Blend.* 23 (July 1989): 10-21, 96.

Bolle, K. W. "Myth: An Overview." *The Encyclopedia of Religion.* 1987 ed.

Brenner, C. *An Elementary Textbook of Psychoanalysis.* 1955. Garden City, N.Y.: Anchor Books, 1974.

Bryce, D. *The Mystical Way and the Arthurian Quest.* Wales: Llanerch Enterprises, 1986.

Caldwell, R. *The Origin of the Gods: A Psychoanalytic Study of Greek Theogonic Myth*. Oxford: Oxford University Press, 1989.

Campbell, J. *The Flight of the Wild Gander: Explorations in the Mythological Dimension*. 1951. Washington, D. C.: Gateway Editions, 1969.

———. *The Hero's Journey. Joseph Campbell: On His Life and Work*. Ed. P. Cousineau. San Francisco: Harper & Row, 1990.

———. *The Hero with a Thousand Faces*. 1949. Princeton: Princeton University Press, 1973.

———. *The Inner Reaches of Outer Space: Metaphor as Myth and as Religion*. New York: Perennial Library, 1986.

———. Interview. "Man and Myth: A Conversation with Joseph Campbell." With S. Keen. *Psychology Today*, 5.2 (July 1971): 35-39, 86-91, 94-95.

———. *The Masks of God: Creative Mythology*. 1968. New York: Penguin Books, 1976.

———. *The Masks of God: Primitive Mythology*. 1959. New York: Penguin Books, 1987.

———. *The Mythic Image*. Princeton: Princeton University Press, 1974.

———. *Myths to Live By*. 1972. New York: Bantam Books, 1988.

———. *An Open Life*. Eds. J. M. Mather and D. Briggs. New York: Larson Publications, 1988.

———. *The Power of Myth*. Ed. B. S. Flowers. New York: Doubleday, 1988.

———. *Transformations of Myth Through Time*. New York: Perennial Library, 1990.

———. *The Way of the Animal Powers*. Vol. 1, Pt. 1 of *Historical Atlas of World Mythology*. New York: Harper and Row, 1988.

Childs, B. *Myth and Reality in the Old Testament.* London, 1960.

Colegrave, S. *Uniting Heaven and Earth: A Jungian and Taoist Exploration of the Masculine and Feminine in Human Consciousness.* Los Angeles, CA.: Tarcher, 1979.

Desai, M. *The Gospel of Selfless Action or The Gita According to Gandhi.* Ahmedabad: Navajivan Publishing House, 1946.

Doty, W. G. *Mythography: The Study of Myths and Rituals.* University: University of Alabama Press, 1986.

Downing, C. "Masks of the Goddess: A Feminine Response." *Paths to the Power of Myth: Joseph Campbell and the Study of Religion.* Ed. D. C. Noel. New York: Crossroad, 1990.

Edmunds, L. ed. *Approaches to Greek Myth.* Baltimore: The John Hopkins University Press, 1990.

Eisner, R. *The Road to Daulis: Psychoanalysis, Psychology, and Classical Mythology:* Syracuse University Press, 1987.

Eliade, M. *Myth and Reality.* Trans. W. R. Trask. New York: Harper and Row, 1963.

___. *Rites and Symbols of Initiation.* 1958. New York: Torchbooks, 1975.

Ellis, T. P., and J. Lloyd, trans. *The Mabinogion II.* Oxford: Clarendon Press, 1929.

Feinstein, D. "The Inner Quest: Bringing a Mythological Perspective to Psychotherapy." *Common Boundary*, 8.1 (Jan-Feb 1990): 18-22.

___. "Personal Mythology: An Interview with David Feinstein." *Magical Blend*, 23 (July 1989): 37-43.

Fontenrose, J. *The Ritual Theory of Myth.* Berkeley: University of California Press, 1966.

Fox, M. *The Coming of the Cosmic Christ: The Healing of Mother Earth and the Birth of a Global Renaissance*. San Francisco: Harper and Row, 1988.

Frappier, J. *Chrétien de Troyes: The Man and His Work*. Trans. R. J. Cornier. 1968. Athens, Ohio: Ohio University Press, 1982.

Frazer, J. G. *The Golden Bough: The Roots of Religion and Folklore*. 1890. New York: Avenel Books, 1981.

Freud, S. "Creative Writers and Day-Dreaming." 1907. In *Standard Edition* 9. Ed. James Strachey. London: Hogarth Press. 1975

___. "The Ego and the Id." 1923. *SE* 19. Ed. J. Strachey., 1975.

___. "Leonardo Da Vinci and a Memory of His Childhood." 1910. *SE* 11. Ed. J. Strachey., 1975.

Frey-Rohn, L. *From Freud to Jung: A Comparative Study of the Psychology of the Unconscious*. Trans. F. E. Engreen & E. K. Engreen. 1974. Boston, Mass.: Shambhala, 1990.

Frye, N. *Anatomy of Criticism*. Princeton: Princeton University Press, 1957.

Geffken J. "Euhemerism." *Encyclopedia of Religion & Ethics*. n.d.

Glut, D. F. (Based on a story by George Lucas). *Star Wars: The Empire Strikes Back*. New York: Del Ray, 1980.

Gordon, A. "*Return of the Jedi*: The End of the Myth." *Film Criticism*. 8.2 (Winter 84): 45-54.

___. "*The Empire Strikes Back* Monsters from the Id." *Science-Fiction Studies*. 7.3 (Nov. 80): 313-18.

___. "The Power of the Force: Sex in the *Star Wars* Trilogy." *Eros in the Mind's Eye: Sexuality and the Fantastic in Art and Film*. Ed. D. Palumbo. New York: Greenwood Press, 1986.

Gresseth, G. K. "The Gilgamesh Epic and Homer." *Classical Journal*, 70.4 (Apr-May 1975): 1-18.

Guest, C. trans. *The Mabinogion*. 1877. London: John Jones Cardiff, 1977.

Gunkel, H. *Genesis*. 4th ed. Göttingen, 1917. n.p.

Guyer, F. E. *Chrétien de Troyes: Inventor of the Modern Novel*. New York: Bookman Associates, 1957.

Hamilton, E. *Mythology*. Boston: Little, Brown, and Co., 1942.

Harding, M. E. *The I and the Not-I: A Study in the Development of Consciousness*. 1965. Princeton: Princeton University Press, 1973.

___. *Psychic Energy: Its Source and Its Transformation*. 1947. Princeton: Princeton University Press, 1973.

Heffernan, C. F. "Chrétien de Troyes' *Yvain*: Seeking the Fountain." *Res Publica Litterarum: Studies in the Classical Tradition*. 5.1 (1982): 109-121.

Hinkle, B. M. "An Introduction to Analytic Psychology." In *An Outline of Psychoanalysis*. Ed. J. S. Van Teslaar. New York: Modern Library, 1925.

Hoeller, S. A. "Jung and the Occult." *Gnosis*, 10 (Winter 89): 22-27.

Jacobi, J. *Complex Archetype Symbol in the Psychology of C. G. Jung*. Trans. R. Manheim. 1957. Princeton: Princeton University Press, 1974.

Jacobsen, T. *The Treasures of Darkness: A History of Mesopotamian Religion*. New Haven: Yale University Press. 1976.

Johnson, R. A. *Inner Work*. San Francisco: Harper & Row. 1986.

Jung, C. G. *Aion*. Vol. 9, Pt. 2 of *Collected Works*. Princeton: Princeton University Press, 1978.

———. "Analytical Psychology and *Weltanschauung*." 1960. *CW* 8. Princeton: Princeton University Press, 1978.

———. *The Archetypes and the Collective Unconscious. CW* 9.1. Princeton: Princeton University Press, 1977.

———. ed. *Man and His Symbols.* 1964. New York: Laurel, 1984.

———. *Memories, Dreams, and Reflections.* Ed. A. Jaffé. Trans. R. and C. Winston. New York: Vintage Books, 1965.

———. *Mysterium Coniunctionis. CW* 14. Princeton: Princeton University Press, 1977.

———. *The Spirit in Man, Art, and Literature. CW* 15. Princeton: Princeton University Press, 1978.

———. *Symbols of Transformation. CW* 5. Princeton: Princeton University Press, 1976.

———. *Two Essays on Analytical Psychology. CW* 7. Princeton: Princeton University Press, 1972.

———. and C. Kerenyi. *Essays on a Science of Mythology.* 1949. Princeton: Princeton University Press, 1973.

Kahn, J. (Based on a story by George Lucas). *Star Wars: Return of the Jedi.* New York: Del Ray, 1983.

Kenna, M. E. "Anthropological Approaches to the Study of Myth." *Didaskalos*, 3 (1971): 520-535.

Keyes, K. *Handbook to Higher Consciousness.* Living Love Center: Coos Bay, Oregon. 1975.

Kirk, G. S. *Myth: Its Meaning and Functions in Ancient and Other Cultures.* 1970. Berkeley: University of California Press, 1973.

Knaster, M. "Raider of the Lost Goddess." *EastWest*, 20.12 (December 1990): 36-43.

Knox, B. "The Enduring Myths of Ancient Greece." *The Classical Outlook*, 62.4 (1985): 118-21.

Kolokithas, D. "Symbols of Transformation." *Gnosis*, 10 (Winter 1989): 10-12.

Leeming, D. A. *Mythology: The Voyage of the Hero*. Philadelphia: J. B. Lippincott, 1973.

Loomis, R. S. *Celtic Myth and Arthurian Romance*. New York: Columbia University Press, 1927.

Lucas, G. *Star Wars: The Adventures of Luke Skywalker*. New York: Ballantine Books, 1976.

Malinowski, B. *Myth in Primitive Psychology*. 1926. New York; Magic, Science and Religion, 1955.

Matthews, C. *Arthur and the Sovereignty of Britain: King and Goddess in the Mabinogion*. London, England: Arkana, 1989.

Middleton, J. ed. *Myth and Cosmos: Reading in Mythology and Symbols*. New York: The Natural History Press, 1967.

Morford, M. P. O., and R. J. Lenardon. *Classical Mythology*. 1971. 2nd ed. New York: Longman, 1977.

Mullahy, P. *Oedipus: Myth and Complex, A Review of Psychoanalytic Theory*. 1948. New York: Grove Press, 1955.

Neumann, E. *Amor and Psyche: The Psychic Development of the Feminine*. 1952. Princeton: Princeton University Press, 1973.

___. *The Origins and History of Consciousness*. 1954. Princeton: Princeton University Press, 1970.

Norman, D. *The Hero: Myth/Image/Symbol*. New York: The World Pub. Co., 1969.

Patai, R. *Myth and Modern Man*. Englewood Cliffs. New Jersey: Prentice-Hall, 1972.

Rama, S. *Perennial Psychology of the Bhagavad Gita.* 1972. Honesdale, Penn: Himalayan International Institute, 1988.

Ramacharaka, Y., trans. *Bhagavad Gita.* Desplaines, Illinois: The Yogi Publication Society, 1930.

Rank, O. *The Myth of the Birth of the Hero.* 1932. New York: Vintage Books, 1964.

Rieder, J. "Embracing the Alien: Science Fiction in Mass Culture." *Sci-Fiction Studies,* 9.1 (Mar. 1982): 26-37.

Rizzuto, A. *The Birth of the Living God: A Psychoanalytic Study.* Chicago: The University of Chicago Press, 1979.

Roberts, B. F. "The Welsh Romance of the *Lady of the Fountain (Owein).*" *The Legend of Arthur in the Middle Ages.* Eds. P. B. Grout, et al. Cambridge, England: D. S. Brewer, 1983.

Sandars, N. K., trans. *The Epic of Gilgamesh.* 1960. Middlesex, England: Penguin Books, 1987.

Sanford, J. A. *The Invisible Partners.* New York: Paulist Press, 1980.

Satchidananda, S. S. *The Living Gita.* New York: Henry Holt & Co. 1988.

Stone, S. ed. *The Esalen Catalog.* California: Esalen Institute, 27.2 (May-Oct 1988).

Taimni, I. K. *Man, God and the Universe.* Wheaton, ILL.: The Theosophical Publishing House (A Quest Book). 1969.

Tigay, J. H. *The Evolution of the Gilgamesh Epic.* Philadelphia: University of Pennsylvania Press, 1982.

Toppings, E. Introduction. *The Age of Fable: Bulfinch's Mythology.* By T. Bulfinch. New York: Armont Publishing Co., 1965.

Vickery, J. B. Ed. *Myth and Literature: Contemporary Theory and Practice*. Lincoln: University of Nebraska Press, 1966.

von Franz, M-L. *Projection and Re-Collection in Jungian Psychology: Reflections of the Soul*. 1978. Trans. W. H. Kennedy. London: Open Court, 1980.

Villela-Minnerly, L., and R. Markin. "*Star Wars* as Myth: A Fourth Hope?" *The Psychoanalytic Review*, 74.3 (Fall 1987): 387-99.

Waller, M. "Poetic Influence in Hollywood: *Rebel without a Cause* and *Star Wars*." *Diacritics*, 10 (Sept. 1980): 57-66.

Watts, A. W. "Western Mythology: Its Dissolution and Transformation." *Myths, Dreams, and Religion*. Ed. J. Campbell. 1970. Dallas: Spring Publications, 1988.

Weber, R. "Plato's Ladder of Love." In *A Spiritual Approach to Male/Female Relations*. Ed. S. Miners. Wheaton, III.: The Theosophical Publishing House (A Quest Book), 1984.

Wilber, K. *Eye to Eye: The Quest for the New Paradigm*. Garden City, New York: Doubleday, 1983.

___. *No Boundary: Eastern and Western Approaches to Spiritual Growth*. Boston: Shambhala, 1979.

___. *The Spectrum of Consciousness*. 1977. Wheaton, Illinois: Quest, 1985.

Worthington, V. *A History of Yoga*. 1982. London, England: Arkana, 1989.

Wundt, W. M. *Volkerpsychologie*. Leipzig: W. Englemann, 1914.

Wyatt, D. "Star Wars and the Productions of Time." *Virginia Quarterly Review*, 58.4 (Autumn 1982): 600-15.

The Reshaping of Psychoanalysis
From Sigmund Freud to Ernest Becker

This series is designed to offer works which are concerned with the reshaping and revitalization of psychoanalysis. Also critical to this series is the interweaving of such disciplines as psychology, psychiatry, religion, and philosophy so as to promote dialogue and offer avenues toward rapprochement.

This series will publish and proffer studies of Freud and Neo-Freudians such as Becker which are most aware of the long term contributions of psychoanalysis toward the healing of self and society. Studies should be scholarly and clinically discerning. This is a series which is keenly concerned with the bridging of disciplines, the networking of ideas and peoples, and with the perpetuation of the psychoanalytic questions, and, at times, its answers. This is a series which is also very open to its authors' creativity and most appreciative of those efforts which reshape, revamp, revitalize, and transform Freudian psychoanalysis.

The General Series Editor is Barry R. Arnold, an Emory Ph.D., who is Associate Professor of Religious Studies and Philosophy at the University of West Florida. His speciality area is psychoanalysis and medical ethics.